The Acquittal of God

THE ACQUITTAL OF GOD

A Theology for Vietnam Veterans

Uwe Siemon-Netto

PILGRIM PRESS
NEW YORK

Biblical quotations, unless otherwise noted, are from the Revised Standard
Version of the Bible, copyright 1946, 1952, © 1971, 1973 by the Division of
Christian Education of the National Council of the Churches of Christ in the
U.S.A., and are used by permission.

Excerpts from *Letters and Papers from Prison*, by Dietrich Bonhoeffer, revised, enlarged edition. Copyright © 1971 by SCM Press, Ltd. Reprinted
with permission of SCM Press, Ltd. and Macmillan Publishing Company.

Excerpts from *Out of the Night: The Spiritual Journey of the Vietnam Vet* by
William Mahedy. Copyright © 1986 by William Mahedy. Reprinted by
permission of Ballantine Books, a Division of Random House, Inc.

Design by Publishers' WorkGroup

Cover photograph: United Press International

Library of Congress Cataloging-in-Publication Data

Siemon-Netto, Uwe.
   The acquittal of God : a theology for Vietnam veterans / Uwe
Siemon-Netto
      p.   cm.
   Bibliography: p.
   ISBN 0-8298-0833-7
   1. Vietnamese Conflict, 1961-1975—Veterans—United States.
2. Veterans—United States—Religious life. 3. Bonhoeffer,
Dietrich, 1906-1945. 4. Suffering—Religious aspects—Christianity.
I. Title.
DS559.73.U6S54   1989
208'.697—dc20   89-35816
                                                          CIP

The Pilgrim Press, 475 Riverside Dr., New York, NY 10115

Dedicated to
the Veterans of the Vietnam War

Contents

Foreword 9

Preface 11

Introduction 13

1. The Stolen Time 23

2. Encountering Evil 33

3. Making Choices 42

4. Where America Failed Its Veterans 53

5. Good from Evil 62

6. Making Sense of the Veterans' Pain 68

7. A World Come of Age 77

8. The Communion of Saints 83

9. Conclusion 93

Notes 97

Selected Bibliography 105

Foreword

This book is an astonishing event. Uwe Siemon-Netto experienced a world seldom if ever accessible to a theologian, a world of indescribable physical and psychological destruction. Over a period of five years he spent countless days with soldiers in a dirty jungle war. He was with them when they tried to stay alive, torched villages, were ambushed, and when they found it necessary to kill civilians. He was with them when their helicopters were shot down, when they were wounded, when they died. They confided their loves, hatreds, hopes, and despair to this foreign correspondent. They considered him one of them, for his life was as much at risk as theirs.

When it was over, he was unable to forget his experience of solidarity with the participants of this war, with their actions and with the negative results of those actions. He has no intention of forgetting. He chose to be with them as they suffered, back home, from the humiliations of Vietnam. He is with them in their isolation as they desperately try to shake off the cataclysm others conveniently overlooked. The journalist-turned-theologian worked with these men as chaplain and therapist, trying to help them discover why all this has happened to them and what their mission is.

In the midst of a forgetful America, Siemon-Netto discovered Dietrich Bonhoeffer's visions. They are the visions of a man who in his last years practiced solidarity with the rejected, the victims of the heaven-storming nihilists and murderers of the Nazi era in Germany. And this encounter has helped to create hope for the hardened ex-GIs who felt cheated of all hope of bringing meaning and usefulness to their lives.

Uwe Siemon-Netto realized that the theology of suffering that Bonhoeffer developed in his last years of imprisonment holds great promise for these forgotten and rejected veterans—the promise of a task to be accomplished in an America which claims to be Christian.

And so Siemon-Netto works his way through various statements in Bonhoeffer's essay "After Ten Years" and his *Letters and Papers from Prison*. As a result, exciting intellectual analyses of these texts alternate with the emotional and committed narration of the lives of comrades-in-suffering—the lives these GIs lived then and have to live now even when they find it almost impossible to live.

It is only natural that in this endeavor he occasionally tests the limits to which Bonhoeffer can be used. They are the limits of a daring application of Bonhoeffer's observations and conclusions to the experiences of veterans in the American society of the 1970s and 1980s. But a journey has begun. It is a journey for which encouraging objectives are given to the Vietnam veterans in their depressing situation.

With suspense we await the vistas that will open as the next twists and turns of this journey are navigated.

EBERHARD BETHGE

Preface

When journalists find themselves on a difficult assignment they naturally wonder, "What am I doing here?" I asked myself this question time and again in my five years as a correspondent in Vietnam. What was I doing in somebody else's war? What was I doing exposing myself to mortar rounds, rockets, sniper fire, punji sticks poisoned with human feces, amoebas, malaria, liver worms? What was I doing staring into a mass grave in Hue? What was I doing in a foxhole holding the hand of a mortally wounded GI?

"What am I doing here?" I said to myself when years later I attended a cocktail party in New York and listened to a young socialite calling Vietnam veterans "my least favorite minority."

"What am I doing here?" I asked when at the age of fifty I was a junior seminarian at the Lutheran School of Theology at Chicago. What was a journalist with a penchant for secular pleasures doing in a seminary?

Then one day I attended a briefing on Clinical Pastoral Education and heard myself ask, "Do VA hospitals take CPE students?" And when in the summer of 1987 I worked as a "chaplain intern" at the Veterans Administration Medical Center in St. Cloud, Minnesota, I ceased asking myself, "What am I doing here?"

I knew that I was witnessing a phenomenon of historical importance. I was given a glimpse of the deep despair of men who as teenaged soldiers and now as middle-aged veterans had suffered unprecedented darkness and estrangement. As I counseled them privately and worked with them in "rap groups" it became clear to me that I was dealing with a group of men whose pain was preparing them for a pivotal role in the destiny of the country which had sent them out to die and then rejected them when they returned with wounded souls and bodies.

This experience has been the most important in my professional life. I feel humbled by the veterans' trust in me. And I am grateful that I was able to talk with these men, who feel so estranged from the Ground of Being, about Dietrich Bonhoeffer's theology of God's suffering for us.

I owe special thanks to Eberhard Bethge for suggesting that I apply Bonhoeffer's essay "After Ten Years" to the veterans' plight. My thanks are also due to William P. Mahedy for the deep theological insights as well as the wealth of other information in his magnificent book *Out of the Night* which has an important place in this thesis.

I am thankful to all the veterans in Minnesota I have worked with, but especially to the Brainerd rap group for reading "After Ten Years" and then discussing it with me. I thank my friend Lenny Roberts, a maintenance foreman at LSTC, for confiding to me the pain and anguish he experienced while a marine in Vietnam and, especially, after his return to the United States. I am very grateful to Dr. Arthur Kuhne and Dr. James Tuorila, two remarkable VA psychologists, for their advice and cooperation. The same goes for Gary Berg and Arthur Ree, chief of chaplains and Clinical Pastoral Education supervisor, respectively, at the Veterans Administration Medical Center at St. Cloud.

I should like to express my heartfelt appreciation to F. Burton Nelson of North Park Theological Seminary, under whose scholarly guidance I studied Bonhoeffer's life, theology, and ethics, and to Kurt Hendel who, as my advisor at LSTC, greatly facilitated my somewhat unusual course of studies. I am deeply indebted to LSTC's three professors of systematic theology, Carl E. Braaten, Robert W. Bertram, and Philip Hefner, who taught me to think theologically. My thanks are also due to Franklin Sherman for his advice and to Paul Bauermeister for briefing me on pastoral care and psychological aspects.

I am forever grateful to my pastor, John S. Damm of St. Peter's Church in New York City, for inspiring me to study theology and paving my way to LSTC, and I thank the congregation of St. Peter's for its spiritual support. Most of all, I thank my wife, Gillian, for her patience with me and her support when I suddenly interrupted my career as a journalist to study theology. She was the first one to read every new chapter, and she proved to be a wonderful critic.

Introduction

SUFFERING
ACROSS ETHNIC BARRIERS

"Where was God when we went through hell in Vietnam?" a veteran asked in group therapy. "He was smart, he went AWOL," another former soldier replied.

The military acronym AWOL stands for "Absent Without Leave." In times of war it is a very serious offense punishable by imprisonment or even death.[1] Vietnam veterans often express the conviction that the Almighty deserted them in the jungles and rice paddies of Indochina. They believe that God has stayed away from them ever since, and that that is why they are still suffering.

This volume is a plea for God's acquittal of the charge of desertion. To view suffering as evidence of God's absence is to misunderstand the essence of the Christian faith. Malcolm Muggeridge sees suffering as the only method by which we have ever learned anything. God does not will our pain, which is part of the human condition; God does not delight in it. Far from deserting us, God will turn suffering to our benefit. "God will bring good out of evil, even out of the greatest evil," wrote Dietrich Bonhoeffer shortly before he was hanged by the Nazis.

From this premise Christians may expect astonishing results from the pain of the Vietnam veterans. In the history of the United States, no other cross-cultural group of Americans has suffered as much and for as long as these men and, to a considerable extent, their families. Of course, blacks, American Indians, and Asians, and the legions of battered women and abused children of all races and income groups have suffered. Yet they do not represent the whole spectrum of this country's population. The Civil War, which caused half a million deaths, brought tremendous suffering. But in its aftermath the pain in the North was largely limited to the grief over the loss of sons, whereas only the South felt the agonies older nations around the world have had to live with at one point or another in their history, the agonies of defeat, humiliation, and disgrace—the penalties of the vanquished.

The Vietnam veterans have suffered all of the above and more. They may well have been the first soldiers in history to be rejected, spat upon, and insulted by the civilian population of their own country. They were doubtless the only ones to have been turned away by churches and turned down by the opposite sex for no other reason than their service in an unpopular war, a service most of them had to perform by force of law.

After their defeat in World War II, German soldiers also continued to suffer. But when they returned to their devastated country, they met fellow-sufferers. Their wives, sisters, parents, and children had experienced nightly air raids, the terror of the totalitarian system, starvation, flight, foreign occupation, the division of their country, in many cases the loss of their homeland, and the collective shame over the crimes an evil regime had committed in their name. Thus in Germany veterans and civilians shared the same fate and were compelled to bear jointly the burden with which they had been left.

Vietnam veterans, by contrast, returned to the uncomprehending beneficiaries of a booming economy. From the mud and the blood in Vietnam's jungles they returned to the land of mini-skirts and flower power; they returned to a self-indulgent society whose motto was "Do your own thing." They returned to a nation experimenting with "mind-expanding" drugs as a substitute for God, a nation with a limited attention span, a nation unwilling to live with unpleasant memories. As Vietnam veterans tell it, they were ostracized because their fellow-countrymen did not wish to be reminded by their presence of what Americans saw as a national embarrassment.

A FATE OF MILLIONS

This kind of rejection combined with combat experience and the thought of having risked death and mutilation in vain has caused intense suffering to literally millions of Americans in the prime of their lives. Of the nearly 2.8 million U.S. military personnel who served in Vietnam, 1.6 million were in combat areas. Almost 58,000 died in that war. An equal number have either committed suicide or lost their lives under other than natural circumstances since their return to the United States.[2]

Of the surviving veterans, it is estimated that between 700,000 and 1.5 million are "in need of emotional help."[3] Veterans Administration (VA) psychologists work on the assumption that 800,000 currently are suffering from post-traumatic stress disorder (PTSD), a newly discovered malady whose symptoms were previously inadequately described as shell shock or combat fatigue.[4] To what extent wives, children, and other relatives of veterans are also suffering is only now being studied. Therapists in three different Veterans Administration medical centers have told me that two-thirds of their Vietnam-era patients have one or several divorces behind them. One patient in North Chicago has married and divorced nine wives since returning from the war. All therapists interviewed attributed this marital instability to the veterans' inability to "get close" to another person for fear of losing that person as they have lost their best friends in combat.

The war was fought mainly by adolescents. The average age of the soldiers was nineteen, compared with an average age of twenty-five in World War II;[5] two-thirds of the men killed in action were younger than twenty-one years of age.[6] In Vietnam they faced a foe quite unlike the enemies previous GIs had fought. In five years of covering the war, I often witnessed the North Vietnamese practices of using women and children as combatants and of booby-trapping babies as well as the bodies of fallen Americans. All this was clearly part of their strategy and not some isolated atrocity. And it was the kind of cruelty young American soldiers were not prepared for.

STRENGTH THROUGH PAIN

Dietrich Bonhoeffer did not live to see the day when thousands of American men chose to vegetate in their private war zones in otherwise benign forests, because they found it impossible to reintegrate into a society that rejected them for no other reason than that they had complied with the law and served in their country's armed forces. Bonhoeffer could not know that hundreds of thousands of former soldiers would resort to drug and alcohol abuse as a "kind of self-medication against PTSD."[7] Bonhoeffer, a psychiatrist's son, probably could not even imagine what post-traumatic stress disorder was, for this complaint was not discovered until some twenty years after his death, when it was called "KZ syndrome."[8] It manifests itself in flashbacks, nightmares, difficulties in maintaining steady relationships with other human beings, feelings of alienation, survival guilt, sleep disturbance, and the inability to concentrate. According to J. Ingram Walker and Jesse O. Cavenar, it is present in 40 to 50 percent of all Vietnam veterans.[9]

But Dietrich Bonhoeffer had probably deeper insights into the phenomenon and meaning of suffering than any other theologian of this century. He made suffering the central part of his theology,[10] and prompted others, notably Jürgen Moltmann, to pursue this theme in great depth. It was Bonhoeffer who wrote,

> We have to learn that personal suffering is a more effective key, a more rewarding principle for exploring the world in thought and action than personal good fortune.[11]

This is not, of course, an exclusively theological wisdom. In the Bordeaux region of France the first thing every aspiring young man learns before setting out to become a vintner is the time-honored wisdom, la vigne doit souffrir (the vine must suffer), for the more the vine thirsts in an arid vineyard full of pebbles, the deeper its roots must burrow into the ground searching for moisture. This gives strength to the branches and causes them to produce the rich grapes which account for the superb quality of the red Bordeaux wines.

That suffering is essential for growth is thus a verity that transcends even the boundaries between species. Where humans are concerned, it has a special significance, however, because evidence suggests that suffering may well be the conduit by which human beings are introduced to the spiritual dimension of their lives. Based upon his experiences in German concentration camps, the Viennese psychologist Victor Frankl has suggested that some people actually benefit from being subjected to extreme stress and pain.[12] According to Frankl they gain a purpose or meaning in life as a direct result of their experiences, and this meaning of life is retained until death if one accepts the challenge to suffer bravely.

A study by Terrence Des Pres of the survivors of the Nazi death camps supports Frankl's theory that, contrary to Freud's Pleasure Principle, striving to find a meaning in life is the primary motivational force within man. This notion was most clearly expressed by a former camp inmate who said, "Life is what counts, life whose internal destiny has had the peace and the time to unfold."[13]

Thus even without reference to any Christian doctrine, the suffering of as large a group as the Vietnam veterans must surely be seen as a momentous event in the history of this young nation; it must have an impact on its future development. I will argue in this volume, however, that a specifically Christian interpretation of this pain will make some sense of it as far as the veterans are concerned and can thus make it more bearable. Furthermore, the agony of the veterans should give their country a new sense of purpose.

STRUGGLING TOWARD MATURITY

Eberhard Bethge, Bonhoeffer's editor and closest friend, in discussing the veterans' plight, has predicted that they will lead America from her state of naiveté, which he termed *charming*, to a state of maturity, which he considered overdue.[14] To give an example of the charming side of America's innocence, he pointed to the honor system in some American universities, a system unthinkable in Europe; but such a system is not part of the real world in which we live, a *mündige Welt*, as Bonhoeffer called it, that is, a world deprived of its innocence. What has happened to the Vietnam veterans, on the other hand, is clearly a feature of this world come of age. In Bethge's eyes their despair was a necessary and major element in the maturing process of their young nation. Consequently, he sees the veterans as a vanguard that will guide a reluctant America to whatever destiny its adulthood will entail.

That thought will be explored in this book, especially in terms of the relationship between hope and the future. Hope is, with faith and charity, one of the three theological virtues. It is, of course, the mature relative of optimism, which along with its opposite, pessimism, Martin Heidegger called a *childish* category. Thus for a nation, as well as for an individual, "coming of age" presupposes the evolution from the stage of optimism to the stage of hope. But just as optimism is the mirror image of pessimism, so hope is the mirror image of despair, which is another category of the mature, and a basic condition in which hundreds of thousands of Vietnam veterans live. The task is therefore to somehow convert their despair to hope.

It was Eberhard Bethge who suggested applying Bonhoeffer's insights in "After Ten Years" to the veterans' despair, in order to interpret those insights for the benefit of not only the sufferers themselves but the world at large.[15] Thus I sent that article, which now appears as the prologue to Bonhoeffer's *Letters and Papers from Prison*, to a group of Vietnam veterans in Brainerd, Minnesota. The group read and later discussed it. Rap groups seem to be the preferable form of treatment for PTSD. According to psychiatrist Robert Jay Lifton, one of the leading experts on PTSD, the rap groups came into being "because the veterans sensed that they had more psychological work to do in connection with the war. It is important to emphasize that the veterans themselves initiated the groups. The men . . . wanted to understand what they had been through, begin to heal themselves, and at the same time make known to the American public the human costs of the war."[16]

Rap groups are thus made up of what may be considered an elite among the suffering veterans, an elite in the sense that they are trying to pull themselves out of their despair and, in the words of Walker and Cavenar, "understand their role in the war more clearly and take responsibility for their personal behavior during and after the war."[17]

In Brainerd, I was given the rare opportunity to tape the group's discussion of the Bonhoeffer text. This lasted almost three hours and turned out to be so intense that the veterans did not even stop for their habitual "smoke break." Although Bonhoeffer wrote his essay in another era and for a different readership, one that was confronted with a different set of problems, the veterans were fascinated by the topics he addressed. They identified with the implications of his subtitles, for example, "No ground under our feet," "Who stands fast?" "Of folly," "Contempt for humanity?" "Of suffering," "Are we still of any use?" and "The view from below." I have incorporated some of the views expressed during that session into the body of this book, in which I attempt to match each section of "After Ten Years" with the experiences of the Vietnam veterans and issues and insights relating to them.

In the discussion, the veterans were uninhibited by my presence and microphone because I had worked with this group in the summer of 1987 while serving as a chaplain intern in the Veterans Administration Medical Center in St. Cloud, Minnesota. I regard it as a privilege to have been accepted by the group as a peer, although I have never been a soldier. I did, however, spend five years in Vietnam as a war correspondent for German newspapers; I often accompanied the troops into combat; I was with them when they were maimed, when they died, or when they had no choice but to shoot at women and children who were used as combatants by the enemy. I know from personal experience what veterans mean when they talk about their flashbacks and nightmares, and their inability to bond—all of which are symptoms of PTSD.[18]

The Brainerd group consisted of, at various times, between ten and twenty men, all of extraordinary character. There was, for example, an officer whom I had met in early 1965 in Binh Dinh province where he served as an advisor to a senior South Vietnamese commander. After his return to the United States he unsuccessfully ran for Congress, taught political science at the college level, and dedicated a considerable amount of his time to Indochinese refugees. He helped them as they tried to integrate into their new American environment, and, more importantly, he tried to persuade his fellow-countrymen to open their hearts to these new immigrants.

Then there was a former U.S. Navy corpsman whose job it was to give first aid to Marines who were wounded in combat. He is still haunted by the innumerable instances in which he had to "play God" and put his buddies out of their misery because in his estimation they would not survive anyway. When he came back to America, he found it impossible at first to live among other Americans. For more than a decade he lived in forests, sometimes in an old truck, sometimes just in a sleeping bag, and this in Minnesota winters where temperatures have been known to drop to forty degrees below zero. He has now surfaced and is working on an M.A. in psychology. He was the one who founded the Brainerd group.

There was a former infantryman who was so severely disabled in combat that he spent two years in hospital. Though an invalid, he enrolled in college, majoring in psychology. He is now one of the pillars of his community, a vice-commander of his VFW post, and is heavily involved in helping other veterans. There was a former B-52 pilot who became a magazine publisher, and a marine sergeant who built up a successful construction business and continues to give money to less fortunate comrades. There were veterans who are now farmers and postal workers, and some who are drifters. There were a few who kept winding up in prison for one offense or another.

They all had several things in common. They suffered from PTSD, failed marriages, chemical dependency, and anger. They were angry with God for allowing them to suffer so much, with their fellow-Americans for making them scapegoats for a lost war, and with their government for sending them into a war that, as they saw it, Washington lacked the stamina to win.

They were, with few exceptions, a misogynous body of men. To be sure, most of them had wives or girlfriends, but women were not permitted to attend the rap sessions, and met in their own group instead. The men explained their misogyny by citing bad encounters with the opposite sex during and after their tour of duty in Vietnam. Many combat soldiers received "Dear John" letters from their sweethearts back home informing the men that they did not wish to be associated with "baby killers." According to military attorneys, the frequency and hostility of such letters has never been so high as during the Vietnam war.[19]

THE NEED FOR FORGIVENESS

The term "baby killer" upset veterans more than anything else. Almost all of them heard it within days, if not hours, of their return from combat. Nothing angered them more than hearing it from the pulpits of churches where they had sought solace from a spiritual pain that included remorse over the killing of civilians and, most especially, survival guilt, a phenomenon experienced by former concentration camp inmates as well. The question, why in a catastrophe do some survive while others perish, calls for theological answers. Yet theology is hard to practice with men who accuse God of having forsaken them. In many cases the first sermon they heard after their homecoming prompted them to "flip off" God, as they say in their own, rich jargon.

The Brainerd group was no exception in this regard, nor were two other groups I worked with in Minnesota. Only three of its members still maintained an affiliation with any church; one did so for his son's sake, and the other two found that their suffering actually had strengthened them in their faith. While the others all voiced a belief in God, some thought God had already damned them. They could not understand how God could forgive them if they were incapable of forgiving themselves.

The task at hand, then, is to bring to the veterans the message of forgiveness and reconciliation in order to alleviate their malady, which is rejection and separation. To do this in an accusatory way by stressing the wrongdoings of particular individuals would be a grotesque distortion of the Christian message and would therefore be condemned to failure. As Helmut Thielicke has pointed out in a sermon on the Lord's Prayer, *guilt* is not a private matter; guilt is one's own participation in the "fatality of guilt [*Schuldverhängnis*] brooding over the world, over its continents and seas."[20]

William P. Mahedy, a former U.S. Army chaplain now working with the veterans in San Diego, California, has brought this insight into a contemporary context:

> In theological terms, war is sin. This has nothing to do with whether a particular war is justified or whether isolated incidents in a soldier's war were right or wrong. The point is that war as a human enterprise is a matter of sin. It is a form of hatred for one's fellow human beings. It produces alienation from others and nihilism, and it ultimately represents a turning away from God.[21]

According to Mahedy, "Spiritual darkness as the vets have known it, is really an overpowering awareness of the context of human sin."[22] As will be seen, Bonhoeffer's theology proves very helpful in dealing with this predicament because it provides christological answers. Members of all three rap groups I have worked with proved receptive to the idea that, far from damning them, God suffers with them. They took comfort in the notion that, by what Douglas John Hall calls "Christ's priestly act of solidarity with suffering humanity,"[23] the rejected and suffering God puts an end to man's estrangement, which is sin. As sin is the source of all pain, no pain is too small or too great to qualify for the assurance of that "priestly act of solidarity" that is the very center of the Christian faith.

As hardened citizens of a world come of age, a godless world, the veterans seemed instinctively to understand what Bonhoeffer meant when he wrote, "Man is challenged to participate in the sufferings of God in a godless world."[24] In order to make the veterans see their suffering in this light, however, they must first be made to understand how the suffering God is present among them.

While experiencing the intense spirituality and warmth of the rap groups the thought struck me that they were indeed a congregation, an *ekklēsia,* though they were not yet the church of God whom they have "flipped off." Instead, as a group they seem to be what Paul Tillich described as a latent church of individuals "in whom the Spiritual Presence's impact is felt, although they are indifferent or hostile to all overt expressions of religion."[25]

I believe that the veterans' quest for forgiveness will ultimately transform their "latent church" into what Bonhoeffer described as the *sanctorum communio* in which Christ is present *as* community. Bonhoeffer stressed that due to the universal priesthood of all Christians one member of a congregation can forgive the sins of another. "Of course, only he who has taken the sins upon himself can forgive them, namely Christ," Bonhoeffer wrote, "but this means for us [that Christ's act of forgiving is performed through his presence in] his congregation, as the *sanctorum communio,*" or community of saints.[26]

It is fair to assume, then, that as this is happening, the true meaning of the veterans' pain will become increasingly clear: God did not desert them but calls upon them to help guide their nation to its destiny, to become a leading force in the pursuit of a call that has gone out to all of us. It is the call to suffer with God in a godless world.

1
The Stolen Time

AFTER TEN YEARS

Ten years is a long time in anyone's life. As time is the most valuable thing that we have, because it is the most irrevocable, the thought of any lost time troubles us when we look back. Time lost is time in which we have failed to live a full human life, gain experience, learn, create, enjoy, and suffer; it is time that has not been filled up, but left empty. The last years have certainly not been like that. Our losses have been great and immeasurable, but time has not been lost. It is true that the knowledge and experience that were gained, and of which one did not become conscious till later, are only abstractions of reality, of life actually lived. But just as the capacity to forget is a gift of grace, so memory, by recalling the lessons we have learnt, is also part of reasonable living.[1]

These opening lines of the essay "After Ten Years" were not written to Americans who fought in Vietnam, but to Germans who opposed Hitler. Bonhoeffer wrote this text to commemorate the tenth anniversary of Hitler's rise to power. At Christmas, 1942, he handed copies to his brother-in-law Hans von Dohnanyi and Colonel Hans Oster of the Abwehr, Germany's military intelligence service which actively resisted the Nazis. Both von Dohnanyi and Oster were later executed on Hitler's orders.

Bonhoeffer gave another copy to his closest friend, Eberhard Bethge, who after World War II became the principal editor of his works. In December, 1987, I visited Bethge in his home near Bonn, West Germany, and told him about the veterans' suffering. He immediately replied, "They have had their time stolen from them by

23

the war in Vietnam, and then by uncomprehending civilians back home, just as our time was stolen by Hitler."[2]

While the title "After Ten Years" does not apply literally to the veterans' case—after all, the last American combat soldiers had left Vietnam in 1973, thus sixteen years ago at the time of this writing— Bethge saw many analogies between their situation and that of the Germans opposed to Hitler. Both groups, he said, were deprived of some of their best years, but that need not be "time lost," for both were given unique opportunities to do something for their societies that had never been done before.

Before we deal with these opportunities, it is important to examine whether the "great and immeasurable losses" of the veterans can indeed be interpreted as an asset in the sense that from them knowledge and experience were gained. When the rap group in Brainerd discussed this passage, the following exchange was recorded between the officer (Vet 1), the graduate student of psychology (Vet 2), the undergraduate majoring in psychology (Vet 3), and myself.

Vet 1: In 1972, I wrote . . . , "time, time my mortal enemy." Then the realization—it destroys you—is that you can't accomplish something you want to accomplish. So, like you see, it's a new awareness. Now, here we are, 40, 50 years old, and the time from Vietnam to now is gone. It disappeared on us. When we were young and could do anything we wanted to do, we should have done it.

Siemon-Netto: What should you have done?

Vet 1: Well, my part? Whatever it is—it is different for everyone. But I think we have a lot to tell the public. You know, basically, we were wrong by just walking away from Vietnam and walking away from our responsibilities. And we lost our sense of purpose, our sense of greatness. And I think we have a story and nobody ever told it.

Siemon-Netto: Were you ever encouraged to tell it?

Vet 1: No! No, we faced obstacles if we told it. We were ridiculed.

Vet 2: I tried saying things when I first went to college, when I first came home, and when I first got out of the service. That very fall, I quit the second year because they were demonstrating, and anytime I tried to say anything, all I got was arguments from a bunch of . . . ignorant people that didn't know a goddam thing about what they were talking about. So I left. *I spent fifteen years after that in the . . . woods hating the sons of bitches, you know* [my italics]. I was not encouraged to speak at all.

Vet 3: So, would you say that we didn't really have any choice whether the time was lost or not?

Vet 2: No.

Siemon-Netto: It says here, "Our losses have been great and immeasurable, but time has not been lost. It is true that the knowledge and experience that were gained, and of which one did not become conscious till later, are only abstractions of reality, of life actually lived." How about that knowledge of experience of which you became conscious later?

Vet 2: There are people that are our age who didn't go to Vietnam. They had a different knowledge and experience all through these years. And they seem to be a hell of a lot happier than we are. So I don't know if it's a gain or not. . . .

Vet 1: I doubt if they are happier. They are more ignorant, they are ignorant—

Vet 2: Well, the same ignorance—

Vet 1: Like I said, back in '71, '72, time was my mortal enemy. Later, my feeling was that actually time was so insignificant. . . . You know, we've got to think to get out. So what if it happened ten years ago or if it happens twenty years from now! What's the difference in the history of man? It'll get there. And actually that's why I hit the speaking circuit. I think we all have a lot to share. And I think our experience is a lot more broad than, I'll say, all the naive people running around here who think they control the world's problems by playing like, you know, don't become involved. Just play dead and the problem will go away. I think we know better. And I think we also know that a man must be really a man. We've seen it. . . . We know what it's like to hate somebody or what it's like to kill somebody else. It's not something we are proud of. We don't want to see it again either. . . .[3]

This exchange may stand as a paradigm for two fascinating developments. First, at least for a vanguard of hundreds of thousands of Vietnam veterans the healing process has at last begun, as many therapists, first and foremost William P. Mahedy, have observed.[4] The second development is that the veterans are beginning to make use of their experience. One must not be fooled by their anger. In the final analysis, all three veterans quoted above support Bonhoeffer's view that "the memory, the recalling of lessons we have learnt, is also part of responsible living."

Though only Vet 1 states unequivocally, "We have a lot to tell the public," the others are doing the same thing. Vet 2, who spent fifteen years in the woods, is no longer there, "hating the goddam sons of bitches." Instead, he has reentered society, organizing fellow veterans and preparing for a career as a psychologist. He is still angry, and this occasionally leads to unpleasant encounters with the police; hostility toward authority is, after all, one of the trademarks of these men who feel betrayed by the authorities whose orders they had to follow in Vietnam. Furthermore, Vet 2 still returns to the wilderness where he maintains a mobile home. But he no longer remains there.

Vet 3, probably the angriest of all of them, makes much use of his experience. A severely disabled man, he counsels other veterans and has become heavily involved in the civic affairs of his city and state. He, too, is about to become a psychologist. Working with similar groups of men in San Diego, Mahedy writes:

> I never met a veteran who was willing to relinquish the insights or the altered vision of the world that grew out of his Vietnam experience. The burden of this new worldview is that it must be shared. Returning vets felt that they should exert a profound impact on society. They still believe this. They remain convinced that the American people must allow themselves to be changed by the experiences of their sons and daughters in Vietnam. In the lexicon of Vietnam veterans, resocialization or reintegration always means this kind of reciprocal relationship with society. Veterans are both unwilling and unable to sneak back into their homeland and resume life as if Vietnam had never happened.[5]

NO GROUND UNDER OUR FEET[6]

One may ask whether there have ever before in human history been people with so little ground under their feet.[7]

To make any sense of the previous section of this chapter we must ponder the nature of this Vietnam experience from which the veterans gained their altered vision of the world. It is essential to understand the extent to which the experience is haunting veterans fifteen or twenty years after their return from Indochina.

One day I drove from St. Cloud, Minnesota, to Duluth. En route I stopped for a beer in a little country tavern. Next to me stood a lean man in his late thirties whom I had no trouble identifying as a Vietnam veteran. His body language and his facial expression bespoke defiance. He asked me where I was from and what I was doing there. When I told him that I was working with veterans, he said, "You are looking at one." Then he suddenly grabbed me and cried, "Do you know what I am going through night after night? For twenty years I see in my dreams the face of the first Vietnamese I shot the day I arrived over there. He was an eight-year-old boy."

He had spotted the child as he was riding with his platoon on the back of a truck. "The kid was about to throw a hand grenade onto our vehicle; he had already pulled the pin. My whole platoon would have died. So I blasted him away with my M-16. And now, in my sleep, I see his face as he lay dying, and then I see him as he is ripped to pieces by the explosion of the grenade in his hand. But, you see, now I have twins, and in my dreams the dying boy has my son's face."

The veteran then invited me to his hideout deep in the forest where he said he spent every free hour he had with his sons. He had an all-terrain motorbike; I followed him in my Volkswagen and got stuck. The veteran promised to get his Jeep and pull me out. Half an hour later he returned with his Jeep. He jumped out and pointed a handgun at me. "I want you to get the hell out of here," he said. "I don't want you to come to our tent. I don't want my kids to know that I am a killer."

It took me about twenty minutes to defuse the situation. I explained to him that if he shot me or returned to his tent toting a handgun his sons would indeed see him as a killer. In the end, he handed me the weapon. I secured it, took the ammunition out, returned it to him and suggested he hide it from his children. Suddenly, he fell to his knees and wept. I advised him to join one of my rap groups. But he jumped up, ran to his car, and drove further into the forest.

Later I found out who he was and where he lived. He had served in the same Marine company as a member of the Brainerd group who confirmed the man's story, contacted him, and tried to persuade him to undergo group therapy. He was unsuccessful. The man I met in the bar halfway between St. Cloud and Duluth still has no ground under his feet, and he is but one of tens of thousands, maybe hundreds of thousands, who have effectively left the reality in which the rest of us live.

To have no ground under one's feet is probably the most apt description of post-traumatic stress disorder (PTSD). Its symptoms include:

1. The existence of significant stress
2. Reexperiencing the traumatic event as evidenced by at least one of the following:
   a. Intrusive memories of the event
   b. Recurrent dreams of the trauma
   c. A sudden feeling or acting as if the traumatic event were recurring, triggered by an environmental or emotional stimulus
3. Numbing of experience as evidenced by signs such as:
   a. Diminished interest in activities
   b. Feelings of alienation
4. At least two of the following symptoms that were not present before the trauma:
   a. Exaggerated startle response to stimuli
   b. Sleep disturbance
   c. Survival guilt
   d. Avoidance of activities that arouse recollection of the traumatic event
   e. Intensification of symptoms by exposure to events that resemble the traumatic situation

Walker and Cavenar elaborate, saying

Frequently, Vietnam combat veterans avoid talking about the war and about traumatic dreams, startle reactions, feelings of guilt, and similar symptoms. More often, veterans with post-traumatic stress disorder will [complain] about the difficulty in holding a job or maintaining intimate relationships. They may be unable to assume more than minimal responsibility for themselves and be prone to drug abuse and other illegal activities. Complaints of stress response may appear months or even years after military discharge. Not only do symptoms appear late, but once they are apparent, the veteran delays seeking help because of his characteristic mistrust of authority figures. The Vietnam veteran feels deceived and betrayed by the federal government who asked him to fight for his country and set such limitations on the fighting that it was impossible to win the combat.[8]

New findings indicate that the list of PTSD criteria is incomplete. Several behaviors common among Vietnam veterans are "conspicuously absent" from the list. They include: "anxiety, depression/ perceived helplessness, suicidal ideation, hostility/rage, low frustration tolerance, mistrust, the belief of having been scapegoated, lack of direction and goal orientation, employment difficulties, and illegal activities."[9]

It is far beyond the scope of this volume, which is theological in nature, to enter into an argument over psychological details. However, in order to understand the extent to which these men have lost the "ground under their feet," some of the points raised by van Kampen and by Walker need elaboration. For example, the suicidal ideation shows the very nature of the quicksand in which the veterans see themselves.

In the three rap groups I worked with in Minnesota every member had at one time or another entertained the thought of committing suicide, and several attempted it. One ex-marine was prevented from killing himself when his 12-year-old son caught him on the floor with the muzzle of his Winchester in his mouth and his big toe on the trigger. When in another group in another part of the country suicide was discussed, one veteran, whose job it had been to assassinate communist cadre in Vietnam, offered, in all seriousness, to bring his gun to the next session, shoot any member who desired it, and then kill himself.[10]

It is not difficult to see why Vietnam veterans have "no ground under their feet"—why within five years of their discharge from the military they should have produced such horrible statistics: a death rate exceeding that of other veterans by 45 percent; a suicide rate 72 percent higher; 93 percent more auto fatalities; and 69 percent more Vietnam vets went to prison.[11]

We begin to grasp their despair when we hear stories such as this:

During North Vietnam's 1968 Tet offensive one member of one of my rap groups spent most of his time putting corpses of fallen GIs into body bags. Now he dreams every night that he himself is in a body bag; but the zipper is broken, and the bag cannot be closed.

Another patient, whose task it was to dig up enemy graves so that his commanding officer could report a high body count back to headquarters, dreams of himself in a grave surrounded by Oriental cadavers. Their stench has been with him since the day he returned from Vietnam nearly two decades ago.

A former medic told in a rap group how he was detailed to open body bags and identify the corpses of American troopers. "When I opened the first bag, I saw a buddy who had been the best man at my wedding. I had never touched alcohol before. But after that event I stayed drunk for the rest of my tour of duty in Vietnam." He is now undergoing treatment for alcoholism.

Alcoholism and drug abuse are rampant among the veterans. Veterans Administration therapists now go by the rule of thumb that in 80 percent of all cases "PTSD coexists with alcohol- and drug-related problems," according to William Nohner, himself a combat veteran who is now a counselor in the St. Cloud Medical Center. It is this phenomenon that Arthur Kuhne calls "a kind of self-medication."

The feeling of having no ground under their feet never leaves the veterans, not even when they are asleep. For many, not a night goes by in which they do not wake up trembling and drenched in sweat. Almost all have told their wives, girlfriends, or children never to touch them when they are asleep. Too great is the danger that they might strangle their partners to death as they wake up, believing that they are fighting an aggressor.

During the day, a seemingly irrelevant event can prompt them to lose the ground under their feet. Anything reminding them of Vietnam might trigger a flashback, and suddenly they relive a combat situation. The clatter of helicopter rotors will do it, or a firecracker, a sonic boom, the "wall of heat and humidity hitting you as you leave your air-conditioned apartment in the middle of the summer," the smell of rotten fish, an Oriental face, popping popcorn resembling small-arms fire in the distance, the snarl of a traffic policeman sounding like a gunnery sergeant, the officiousness of an I.R.S.

inspector who suddenly resembles the species most hated by the "grunts"—the "hair-cut light colonels" who bawled them out as they returned from the jungle to their base camps, bawled them out because their hair had grown too long while they were out on an operation.

A flashback doesn't just mean that a veteran suddenly remembers a grisly scene; it means that to all intents and purposes he has left the terra firma of Minnesota, Wisconsin, Oregon, or Kansas, and is back in Vietnam; he has no ground under his feet.

Walker and Cavenar define PTSD as a "response to the fear of annihilation." It is a fear all combatants share. Long before the first U.S. ground forces arrived in Vietnam, R. P. Grinker and J. P. Spiegel wrote about their research of the same phenomenon in World War II veterans. "No matter how strong, stable, or normal a man might be, with sufficient stress he will develop a war neurosis."[12] But as Walker and Cavenar point out, at least five important characteristics set Vietnam veterans apart from the others:

1. **Entering and exiting alone.** For Vietnam veterans there was a lack of the usual unit morale and identification. After training, replacement recruits were shipped separately to Vietnam aboard various commercial jets instead of as a group in ship transport or military aircraft. In Vietnam, the servicemen were rotated frequently during their tour of duty. Keenly aware that the tour of duty was only a year, the goal of combat became one of survival rather than unity to achieve victory.

2. **Opposition at home.** Unprecedented antiwar demonstrations and lack of home support for the war contributed to considerable ambivalence among the troops in Vietnam concerning the necessity of war. The Vietnam veteran felt betrayed and cheated. Upon returning home, the combat-weary veteran discovered that the heroes of the Vietnam war were those who fled across the Canadian border to avoid the draft. A sense of purposelessness about the nature of the war itself became widespread among American servicemen in Vietnam. This sense of purposelessness contributed to mistrust and at times hatred of authority and society; this sense of purposelessness, a major clinical issue, goes beyond specific political values and is derived directly from events in Vietnam.

31

3. The nature of the war. The lack of an all-out attempt to win the war created doubt for the servicemen. There were no front lines, and hard-won territory was given up voluntarily, only to be fought for over and over again. The guerrilla warfare and the enemy's use of women, children, and old men made it impossible to distinguish foe from friend. Infants in baby carriages would be wired with booby traps; young boys would throw hand grenades; beautiful ladies were reported to walk around on the streets shooting American officers with a [Colt] .45. There was no safe haven from the war. The U.S. Embassy in Saigon was attacked time and again; the roads were mined and the trails booby-trapped; restaurants and movie theaters were blown up.

4. Military psychiatry in Vietnam. Lower psychiatric casualty rates in Vietnam were inappropriate indications of successful mental health management. The military claimed that well-trained mental health personnel deployed in Vietnam, the twelve- to thirteen-month combat rotation system, and frequent opportunities for rest and recuperation produced lower psychiatric casualty figures. Later studies, however, demonstrate that the inordinate amount of drug and alcohol use masked symptoms of combat stress. Blank, a psychiatrist who was there, reports that the primary mission of the psychiatrist in the military was to preserve troop strength, not to help individuals.[13]

5. The brief transition period. The return home was rapid and uneasy. Downs reported that he once put a soldier in a helicopter an hour after he had killed someone.[14] Twenty-four hours later he was home.[15] For him there was no gradual comedown, no psychological debriefing, no welcoming party upon return.

If that was not enough to cause the veterans to lose the ground under their feet, being scapegoated certainly was. In Mahedy's words, "Like Pontius Pilate, like Lady Macbeth, the American people washed their hands of the war assuaging their own consciences by treating the veterans as moral outcasts."[16]

2
Encountering Evil

WHO STANDS FAST?

The great masquerade of evil has played havoc with all our ethical concepts. For evil to appear disguised as light, charity, historical necessity, or social justice is quite bewildering to anyone brought up on our traditional ethical concepts, while for the Christian who bases his life on the Bible it merely confirms the fundamental wickedness of evil.[1]

To Dietrich Bonhoeffer, evil appeared disguised as a system that called itself "national socialist." These two adjectives had evoked positive emotions among Germans ten years earlier. The National Socialists, it seemed, had ended the sense of national disgrace they felt from defeat in World War I, the vindictiveness of what Germans called the Versailles *Diktat*, and the economic disaster that resulted in part from that peace treaty. They also provided jobs for millions of unemployed men and women. Like all totalitarian regimes, they developed an elaborate welfare system to compete with the charitable institutions of the church.

To the Vietnam veterans, evil came in a variety of disguises, some of which resembled those of the Nazis. The causes for which North Vietnam claimed to fight would have been recognized by Germans of Bonhoeffer's generation. There was the cause of national pride and unity; there was also the alleged cause of social justice.

Like the Nazis, the North Vietnamese managed to camouflage the real purpose of their struggle, which was the imposition of their totalitarian ideology and system on the noncommunist half of their country, as well as Laos and Cambodia. This purpose was ultimately achieved by a conventional, full-scale invasion in which virtually the entire army of North Vietnam conquered the South. But that happened after U.S. combat troops had already left. While they were there, their enemy conducted the conflict as a "war of national liberation," a euphemism which permitted tactics which after previous wars would have demanded punishment for their perpetrators.

In the conventional conflicts of the past "even soldiers fighting in an unjust war of aggression [were] bound by certain standards of conduct (the German soldiers who invaded Poland in 1939)," writes William P. Mahedy.[2] As the GIs found out in Vietnam, none of these standards applied in a communist "war of liberation," in which terrorism played a key role.

One of the world's foremost experts on revolutionary war is Sir Robert Thompson, who was one of the architects of Britain's victory over communist insurgents in Malaya. He pointed out that it is crucial to understand the relationship between the guerrilla cause and its organization.[3] In most cases, the cause that originally draws people to the guerrilla organization is not love of communism but hatred of foreigners. Many people joined Ho Chi Minh's guerrilla forces from 1946 to 1954 to fight the French. The communists were only one of a host of groups fighting the foreigners; but they were the most ruthless and effective.

Thompson noted that once the original cause has been attained, the key issue is the remaining efficiency of the guerrilla organization. Once the French were gone, the communists had to find new means to rally a population which felt no particular love of communism or hatred of rival national leaders. Terrorism became necessary to maintain organizational discipline and preserve power for the leaders.

It was during one of my first visits to Vietnam, in early 1965, that I found out how communist guerrilla groups use terrorism to effect their purposes. I accompanied a South Vietnamese battalion to a village the Vietcong had raided the previous night. Dangling from the trees and poles in the village center were the village chief, his wife, and their twelve children, the males, including a baby, with their genitals cut off and stuffed into their mouths, the females with their breasts cut off. The Vietcong had ordered everyone in the village to witness the execution. They started with the baby and then worked their way up to the elder children, to the wife, and finally to the chief himself.

It was all done very coolly, and it was as carefully planned as the destruction of a strategically important bridge in conventional forms of combat. It was an effective way of "winning the hearts and minds" of the rural population—in a cold-blooded act intended to intimidate those who were left. By executing this official and his family in this grisly fashion the communists sent a clear message to the villagers and their mayors in the whole district: This will happen to your families if you don't join our side.

On a national scale, this event was but a minor incident, one of many similar atrocities perpetrated by the Vietcong throughout the country on that same day. To the journalists at the "five o'clock follies," or daily press conference of U.S. and South Vietnamese officials in Saigon, these incidents became a mere statistic no longer worth reporting. What I had witnessed was a routine operation that was typical of phase 2 in a guerrilla war as defined by Mao Zedong, the Chinese Communist leader, and Vo Nguyen Giap, North Vietnam's defense minister.

According to these two strategists, a "war of national liberation" has three phases. In phase 1, "armed agitation and propaganda" occur. In phase 2, the conflict progresses to guerrilla warfare, which includes terror. Phase 3 includes all of the above plus conventional warfare involving regular armed forces in division strength. In Vietnam, this concept was scrupulously followed.

The incident I had witnessed thus differed from the My Lai massacre, the discovery of which was to have a major impact on American public opinion. In My Lai, individual soldiers committed an atrocity in violation of the Pentagon's Rules of Engagement. In Binh Dinh province, Vietcong terrorists carried out government policy. The My Lai murders were the exception, not the rule. As a former medic in one of my rap groups said, "Most men were far too busy fighting and staying alive to fool around killing civilians." The blood bath in Binh Dinh, on the other hand, was but one of countless similar events on that day. Because of their sheer numbers they were impossible to follow up, unless one happened to be on the spot when the misdeed was discovered.

This is why civilians in the United States knew little of the extent of the evil their husbands, sons, sisters, and brothers were confronted with in that incomprehensible war in a distant and unknown land. Even one of the worst communist outrages, the 1968 massacre of some 3,000 civilians in Hue, was largely ignored in America. During the Tet offensive, communist forces came into the former imperial capital with dossiers and photographs of entire families who were to be liquidated. Later I stood at some of the mass graves that contained their bodies still festively dressed for Tet, the lunar New Year. Yet prominent U.S. journalists never bothered to go to the graves. "The television stations, as far as our records show, made no mention of the executions at all, and showed no film reports from Vietnam on the subject."[4]

It is not my purpose to look for the reasons why the important difference between American atrocities, which were always an act of indiscipline, and North Vietnamese cruelties, which were executed by a disciplined force on the orders of a totalitarian government, was so insufficiently stressed by many journalists and other authors writing about Vietnam. Suffice it to say that the resulting fallacies about America's military performance in that country were largely responsible for the appalling way U.S. soldiers were treated when they came home. Thus, members of the Brainerd group nodded approvingly when I read to them what Bonhoeffer had written about "reasonable" people in "Who Stands Fast?"

> With the best intentions and a naive lack of realism, they think that with a little reason they can bend back into position the framework that has got out of joint. In their lack of vision they want to do justice to all sides, and so the conflicting forces wear them down with nothing achieved.[5]

THE WORLD'S PAIN

Like Bonhoeffer and his circle, the Vietnam veterans have no illusions that they can bend back into position the framework that went out of joint in Southeast Asia. Illusions, Mahedy writes, "are no longer possible when one's consciousness has been transformed by personal experience of evil on this scale."[6] The veterans I worked with in Minnesota were tough realists from whose vocabulary the word "dream," which is so frequently uttered in this country, had long been erased. Their encounter with evil was too profound to allow for much self-deception, and here I am referring not only to the evil as evidenced by their enemy's behavior but also to evil done by their own side.

Previous generations of U.S. soldiers also experienced guilt over what they had done in combat. I have met World War II veterans who still have not overcome their horror over killing Germans "who looked like our brothers or cousins." I counseled a former sailor experiencing nightmares over a kamikaze pilot he had shot down; he said the Japanese came so close that he could make out his features, and now he saw them in his dreams. I also worked with a veteran of the Korean war who cannot forget the face of the first North Korean soldier he shot at close range.

But World War II ended in victory for the United States and its allies. The aggressors were defeated. Everybody applauded the returning GIs. What remorse they may have felt was mitigated by the certainty: "I did what I had to do." William Mahedy confirms this: "I have never met an American veteran of World War II who had any doubt that the cause in which he fought was just."[7] Similarly, veterans of the Korean war, though not welcomed home in a ticker tape parade, could take comfort in the thought that they did combat on the side of a significant part of the community of nations. They, too, were spared vilification by their fellow-countrymen.

The Vietnam veterans, on the other hand, had no choice but to face up to the fact that, regardless of who was the aggressor in the conflict, evil deeds were done by men on both sides, for such is the nature of war. There is no question that American leaders devised "monstrously evil strategies for the conduct of the war in the field. The bombing and shelling of villages, the creation of 'free fire zones' in which everything that moved was considered hostile, the use of defoliants, and the adopting of the 'body count' as a criterion of success were all strategies devised by the military high command to satisfy their civilian superiors."[8]

It is beside the point to argue that many of these strategies could have been avoided had not opposition at home prevented the civilian leaders from meeting the enemy on its own turf, that is, in North Vietnam and in neutral Cambodia and Laos where the communists had established their sanctuaries. The fact remains that the Vietnam conflict forced American combatants to face up to the evil on their own side, an evil that touched them personally.

I have encountered many veterans who have been rendered sterile by the Agent Orange dropped on them by American planes in an effort to defoliate the jungle so that enemy units could be spotted from the air. I have met others who were involved in the "fragging" of their own officers because the officers' bravado had, in the eyes of the men, caused too many casualties.[9] Among the twenty members of one of my rap groups, four admitted that they had shot wounded buddies to put them out of their agony. There were also some patients in the Veterans Administration Medical Center who told me that, as helicopter door gunners, they had been involved in a "turkey shoot" of fleeing civilians.

But it is irrelevant here who the aggressor was. As discussed in the introduction, in theological terms, war is Sin because it is a form of hatred for one's fellow human beings. It results in nihilism and ultimately represents a turning away from God. This is not a political statement; politically and even morally a war may well be justified and necessary, and pacifism wrong and harmful. The sin Mahedy is referring to is the human condition that Paul Tillich defines as estrangement from the "Ground of Being." War is an expression of that condition. Soldiers and victims of war experience the sinful side of human nature more acutely than others. As a result, they feel despair and disgust.

In this connection, the Brainerd rap group discussed these lines from Bonhoeffer on "duty":

From the perplexingly large number of possible decisions, the way of *duty* seems to be the sure way out. Here, what is commanded is what is most certain, and the responsibility for it rests on the commander, not the person commanded. But no one who confines himself to the limits of duty ever goes so far as to venture, on his sole responsibility, to act in the only way that makes it possible to score a direct hit on evil and defeat it. The man of duty will in the end do his duty by the devil too.[10]

But then, the soldier in combat has no choices. This is how one member of the Brainerd group reacted to Bonhoeffer's observations about duty:

Yeah, well, the duty thing is just basically what we accepted, and we didn't challenge what was going on. I mean, you just did your job. . . . You could see that what was going on was wrong, and it didn't really feel right while you were over there what you were doing. But you didn't really have any choice in it. You just did it, you know, because that's what you were supposed to be doing. You couldn't really challenge anybody. Who the hell were you going to challenge?

What this man is going through is precisely what psychologist Peter Marin calls "the world's pain," a condition he believes that Vietnam veterans have as no others of our generation: "[It is] the way we internalize and experience as our own the disorder, suffering, and brutality around us."[11]

RECOGNIZING SIN

If "veterans and victims of war experience the sinful side of human nature as few others do,"[12] then the phenomenon of sin needs to be pondered before the meaning of their pain can be analyzed. Paul Tillich explains,

The Augsburg Confession defines Sin as the state of man in which he is "without faith in God and with concupiscence.". . . One could add to these two expressions of estrangement a third one, namely *hubris* . . . , the so-called spiritual sin of pride or self-elevation, which, according to Augustine and Luther, precedes the so-called sensual sin. This gives the three concepts of "unbelief," "concupiscence," and *Hubris* as the marks of man's estrangement.[13]

At this point, we must focus on the first component part of man's estrangement, unbelief, because it provides a useful tool for analysis. "If there were such a word as 'un-faith,' it should be used instead of the word 'unbelief,'" Tillich writes.[14] Indeed, most clergymen and psychologists working with Vietnam veterans confirm that the vast majority of them *believe* in God but no longer have faith in the sense that they trust or love God. Mahedy relates, "They often call God obscene names . . . because they are convinced that He failed them in their moment of greatest need. Our teenaged soldiers of the sixties and seventies, like most Americans, had been led to believe that God would never let them down, that He would always lead them to victory over evil and preserve them in battle against the foe. In Vietnam, it didn't turn out that way. There, young men discovered they'd 'been had,' and they feel terribly betrayed to this day."[15]

It is worth remembering here my goal for this volume, namely, to show that the veterans' despair is a major step in the maturing process of this young nation. This is not to say that suffering has divine purpose in the sense that it is willed by God. As we have seen above, the kind of suffering described here results from Sin; it results from humanity's estrangement from God. But as Bonhoeffer says, "God will bring good out of evil, even the greatest evil." The good that God brings out of suffering is the maturing process. The belief that God always leads Americans to victory over evil and preserves them in battle against the foe marks the believer not as a mature Christian, not as a true man of faith, but as someone in a state of dreaming innocence.

"Who stands fast?" Bonhoeffer asks and then gives himself the answer:

> Only the man whose final standard is not his reason, his principles, his conscience, his freedom, or his virtue, but who is ready to sacrifice all this when he is called to obedient and responsible action in faith and in exclusive allegiance to God—the responsible man, who tries to make his whole life an answer to the question and call of God. Where are these responsible people?[16]

Obviously, there is no point in making one's whole life an answer to the question and call of a God who had, in the perception of so many veterans, "gone AWOL in Vietnam." But there are signs that "the religious dimension of their experience is now beginning to surface," says Gary Berg, chief of chaplains at the VA Medical Center in St. Cloud, Minnesota. There are signs that many of the men whose "faith was badly damaged," according to chaplain Hayward Knight of the North Chicago VA, increasingly show a yearning for some contact with the God they have "flipped off" in Vietnam. Slowly, Vietnam veterans are beginning to realize that God is there and won't "let them off the hook."

During one rap session I asked a group of fifteen veterans whether they wished to "return to normalcy." All of them answered affirmatively. The term "normalcy" meant different things to each of them. But in the final analysis it meant that they all desired a way out of their life of isolation, rage, psychic numbing, alienation, and inability to love and trust others. They desired a healthy relationship with their families and their "higher power"—God.

"They want to be invited back in," says Gary Berg. But barring their return is the awareness that there was something terribly wrong with the God of their childhood, a God who went AWOL in Vietnam. I have found that if there was one theological motif that appealed to veterans, it was that of the rejected and suffering God who by Christ's priestly act of solidarity with suffering humanity put an end to man's estrangement, which is sin. (I return to this motif in my chapter on suffering.) In this context Paul Tillich provides a singularly pertinent thought:

> When the Divine is rejected, It takes rejection upon Itself. It accepts our crucifixion, our pushing away, the defence of ourselves against It. That is the centre of the mystery of Christ. Let us try to imagine a Christ Who would not die, and Who would come in glory to impose upon us His power, His wisdom, His morality, and His piety. He would be able to break our strength, by His wonderful government, by His infallible wisdom, and by His irresistible perfection. But He would not be able to win our hearts. . . . His power would break our freedom; His glory would overwhelm us like a burning, blinding sun; our very humanity would be swallowed in His Divinity. One of Martin Luther's most profound insights was that God made himself small for us in Christ. In so doing, he left us our freedom and our humanity. He showed us His heart, so that our hearts could be won.[17]

William Mahedy echoes this when he writes about God's and man's dilemma in Vietnam: "In Vietnam we were simply living out in vivid terms the consequences of human freedom. We were doing it to ourselves. This is the story of all wars and genocides throughout history. To demand a coercive presence of God restricting our freedom to sin, no matter how horrendously evil the sin might be, is to misunderstand the creation story."[18]

"Who stands fast?" asks Dietrich Bonhoeffer. The answer is evident. Worshipers of a deity that goes AWOL will have no such stamina. Those who stand fast are the followers of the true God who suffers with us for no other reason than to leave us our freedom and humanity. This is not the God of adolescents but of responsible people, a God Vietnam veterans should be able to understand.

3

Making Choices

CIVIL COURAGE?

What lies behind the complaint about the dearth of civil courage? In recent years we have seen a great deal of bravery and self-sacrifice, but civil courage hardly anywhere, even among ourselves.[1]

To stand fast requires a human quality which in German is called *Zivilcourage.* In the English edition of *Letters and Papers from Prison* this term, which plays a major role in Bonhoeffer's thinking, has been translated literally as *civil courage.* To have civil courage means having spine, standing up for one's beliefs. The mark of people with civil courage is that they act according to their convictions. Bonhoeffer even suggested that on certain occasions a show of civil courage is in order even in the face of religious verities. For example, the Gospel's injunctions against taking up the sword did not prevent him from joining a conspiracy to assassinate Hitler. Eberhard Bethge writes, "One evening Bonhoeffer [was asked] what he thought about the New Testament passage, 'All who take up the sword will perish by the sword' (Matt. 26:52). Bonhoeffer's reply was that the word was valid for their circle too—we have to accept that we are subject to that judgment, but that there is now need of such men who will accept its validity for themselves."[2]

In "After Ten Years" Bonhoeffer takes up the theme:

Civil courage, in fact, can grow only out of the free responsibility of free men. . . . It depends on a God who demands responsible action in a bold

**venture of faith, and who promises forgiveness and consolation to the
man who becomes a sinner in that venture.**[3]

The freedom Bonhoeffer is referring to in this context is the flip
side of the freedom whose consequences were acted out in Vietnam
(see chapter 2). It is the freedom to make good use of the suffering
that was the result of the freedom to succumb to the sin of war. As we
shall see in chapter 5, God brings good out of evil. Here we have to
concern ourselves with whether those who have suffered for so long
because of Vietnam are preparing to be God's tool in this endeavor.

If the veterans are to play a major role in the maturing process of
their nation, they will have to muster civil courage. They must
overcome their lack of trust in virtually all non-veterans and in all
institutions. Their trust level has been eroded by what they see as
gross deception on the part of their government, military leaders,
and fellow citizens. To reverse that erosion nothing less than a bold
venture of faith is required.

This should be borne in mind as we read how the Brainerd group
reacted to Bonhoeffer's thoughts on civil courage. The discussion
was preceded by a moving exchange on trust between Vet 1 (the
officer), Vet 2 (the graduate student of psychology), Vet 3 (the
undergraduate student of psychology), Vet 4 (the farmer), Vet 5 (the
builder), and me.

Vet 4: We are just beginning to realize how powerful we really are.
Vet 1: But we're still not unified.
Vet 2: That's a fact.
Vet 4: That's because we've created a whole bunch of loners. . . .
Most of the guys that have been over there are a bunch of loners.
I'm probably just about as bad as they come.
Vet 3: That's right! I agree with you a hundred percent.
Vet 1: Well, I don't think that's all there is. I think we all have
different experiences. So we can't even agree. I go out and I work
with the Vietnamese [refugees]. We were over there risking our
lives for the Vietnamese, and you came back here and you hate the
sons of bitches. I mean, I work with them. So I think the difference is there.

Vet 2: I don't think it's a matter of trust. We have the ability to trust. It's just that who the . . . do you trust?

Vet 5: Well, the point is, does the individual want to take a chance to trust? I mean, I'm finding myself doing it more and more. You're taking a risk. . . . Yeah, it hurts at times. But at other times it doesn't. It's proven to pay off, you know. You have to take a chance, you know. I mean, you said today you're in a class [at college], and you won't even shut your . . . eyes.

Vet 4: Well, you know, we can put up a wall and . . . it's totally impenetrable. And some of them have little peepholes through it to kind of check up on the outside world . . . just to see what the other sucker is up to. Some people like to get periscopes up there and check it all out. But they aren't gonna come out from behind that wall until they're damn sure about what's on the other side of that thing. It's recon, you know. You check out the area before you go jumping into it, because every time we turned around we jumped into something we didn't want to be in and there was nothing we could do about it.

Here, then, lies the parallel between the veterans and Bonhoeffer's allies: Like them, these men have "again and again shown the utmost bravery and self-sacrifice," to use his words. But only now are they "beginning to discover the meaning of the free responsibility of free men" out of which alone civil courage can grow. This is to be borne in mind as we read excerpts from the Brainerd group's discussion on Bonhoeffer's remark on this subject, a discussion that reveals how painful it is to make sense of their experience:

Vet 5: . . . responsibility of free men: You know . . . when you think about it, you weren't free to do anything.

Siemon-Netto: But that was then. What about now—now as a result of your experience?

Vet 5: Now I'm free to make the choices—

Siemon-Netto: Are you now freer . . . more ready to accept freely the responsibility of free men, after what you have been through? Are you freer than, say, a guy who hasn't partaken in your experience?

Vet 5: I would say so . . . free to make the choices, you know, be more alert, I think. . . . That's from my own experience.

Vet 3: I feel the opposite, though, I feel that I've lost my freedom.

Siemon-Netto: But do you think you have lost it for good or are you still working on your freedom?

Vet 3: I'm still working on it to get it back. You know, I don't think it's something that I lost forever, but it seems like it was more of a setback, my experience, than something that would set me free. . . . I'll say I was freer before I ever went into the service. At least I felt freer. I feel right now I am almost a captive of the situation that I've been brought to.

Vet 4: I don't feel responsibility, but I feel that nobody is going to tell me what to do or think ever again. So, I'm free in that sense.

Vet 1: You know, a lot of times when I look back, there was no freedom when I came back. There was a dragging force I couldn't control. It was emotions. It was anger, and it was more like I was on this ship and it was going full blast. I didn't turn it. I mean, it went. And trying to get control of that ship . . . you have no sense of control.

Siemon-Netto: And now Bonhoeffer says, "It depends on a God who demands responsible action in a bold venture of faith, and who promises forgiveness and consolation to the man who becomes a sinner in that venture."

Vet 2: I don't give a . . . if anyone wants forgiveness or consolation. I'll do what the . . . I want to do and when I want to do it.

Vet 4: I'm wondering if forgiveness is not whether God can forgive the soldier and console the soldier, but whether or not the soldier, the combat veteran, can forgive God.

Vet 5: I agree, too, because I felt let down, deserted. . . . It was kind of like a deer hunt, you know.—You get over there, you know, and you experience it first hand. . . . I used to pray all the time that things would get better. . . . And it never came true. And when I got home, my mom had a priest come over to see me because I walked around, and she thought that there was something wrong with me. And, you know, he came to the house and said, "Where is the heathen at?" And he came upstairs and put his hand on my head and pushed me down and said, "Lord, forgive this heathen, for he knows not what he has done. Forgive him, forgive him."

45

But I looked up at him, and he said, "You need forgiveness, son, for you know not what you have done." And I said, "Take your . . . hands off me." And . . . I stood up and pushed my chair back and grabbed him by the hand and said, "Don't you ever touch me again!" And I tell you, from that point I quit going to church for—almost four years, till I got married.

I shall deal more with the insensitivity of clergy to the wounded souls of Vietnam veterans in the discussion of folly in chapter 4. What is interesting here is that some of the veterans have arrived at a crucial stage in a fascinating journey. We shall see that, resentments over their painful experiences notwithstanding, some of them are on the verge of discovering the meaning of "free responsibility of free men."

The discussion in Brainerd reveals a great deal about their journey: The group members recognize that the war and its aftermath had turned them into loners and made them distrustful. But they are no longer functioning as loners. Instead they are a supportive, loving community, a rap group.[4] They are also beginning to recognize that it is time for them to emerge from behind the wall of distrust they have built around themselves.

And while it is still true that they are angry with the God of their childhood, the kind of national deity that never existed, they are willing to take another look at the suffering and rejected God of Christianity; otherwise this distrustful group of men would never have spoken so openly and for so long with a chaplain. And many of them are clearly ready to make use of what they see as their newly acquired freedom "to make the choices," as Vet 5 said. They will display civil courage which grows out of the "free responsibility of free men."

OF SUCCESS

We must take our share of responsibility for the moulding of history in every situation and at every moment, whether we are the victors or the vanquished. One who will not allow any occurrence whatever to deprive him of his responsibility for the course of history—because he knows that it has been laid down on him by God—will thereafter achieve a more fruitful relation to the events of history than that of barren criticism. . . .

To talk of going down fighting like heroes in the face of certain defeat is not really heroic at all, but merely a refusal to face the future. The ultimate question for a responsible man to ask is not how he is to extricate himself heroically from the affair, but how the coming generation is to live. It is only from this question, with its responsibility towards history, that fruitful solutions can come, even if for the time being they are very humiliating. . . . The rising generation will always instinctively discern which of these we make the basis of our actions, for it is their own future that is at stake.[5]

We saw earlier how the group of Vietnam veterans in Brainerd is subtly shifting from a sense of anger and despair to one of civil courage. Though they are still suffering and angry, they are clearly in the process of assuming their share of responsibility in this society. If this were not generally so, their journey would not be referred to as a "journey out of the night [which] is the work of a lifetime."[6]

Having made the assumption that the Vietnam veterans are playing and will further play a key role in the maturing of their nation, we must now look for signs that the veterans are beginning to participate in the molding of history. The Brainerd group gave this particular aspect a great deal of thought, as the following excerpts from their discussion show:

Vet 5: You know, my life has been pretty screwed up with drugs and parties and stuff for almost twenty years or so. I've come to grips with it. I'm able to discuss it with the younger generation, you know, that's inquisitive. I get a lot of people asking about it. And it's, I think it's better for me. I'm more apt to, I guess, forgive and be forgiven, I would have to say.

Siemon-Netto: Bonhoeffer says, "The ultimate question [is] . . . how the coming generation is to live. It is only from this question, with its responsibility towards history, that fruitful solutions can come, even if for the time being they are very humiliating." Does that hit home with anybody?

Vet 3: That's where we are right now.

Siemon-Netto: Go on, elaborate!

Vet 3: You can't understand why the hell you have to go through all that. Now, why couldn't we have left it over there? Why did it have to come home with you? What was the purpose of all that? If there's any meaning to it at all, it has to be that *maybe* you teach the people who have not experienced this situation somehow not to get into it.

Vet 1: What's humiliating about it?

Vet 3: . . . . knowing that I'm not really truly functioning the way I should be.

Siemon-Netto: Do you think you ever will?

Vet 3: I'm hoping so. Now, that's the struggle. . . .

Siemon-Netto: Is that why at your age you are putting yourself through going to school, getting a bachelor's degree, maybe a master's degree, in psychology? Also your involvement with the VFW and—

Vet 3: Well, I lost something when I was over there. And what I lost was, I think, for one thing my youth. . . . One day I was eighteen years old, and the next day I was ninety-six.

Vet 1: . . . You know, when we talk about loss, you lose youth anyway. I mean, they lose it in the drug scene in the States here—

Siemon-Netto: But they have had a choice here.

Vet 1: Yes, partially, but—

Vet 5: There is no "partially." They have a choice here. Wouldn't it have been fun to stay here and make that choice?

Vet 1: Look what you lost. Look what you gained. We had a lot of harsh experiences, right?

Vet 5: Yeah.

Vet 1: Okay. And we're alive, aren't we?

Vet 5: Yeah.

Vet 1: Okay. There's a lot of bodies, and they were killed right here, in the States, driving cars. . . . They lost everything. We came back alive. We've got something to say. We can *do* something. *We can impact on history* [my italics]. We've got experiences other idiots don't have. . . . I say "idiots" because I listen to them talk. They have no concept of reality. They have no concept of what man can do to man. They have no concept of evil. They're naive, they're stupid. You know, when you come back from Vietnam and . . . you walk into a church . . . and this guy's up there preaching about the evils of war. . . . And this guy knows what the hell he's talking about. He's siding with the North Vietnamese who would butcher anybody. . . . I just got up and left. I didn't give him any response.

Vet 2: When I came home, all of a sudden they were demonstrating—right here in Brainerd, professors, priests, and the whole . . . lot.

Vet 1: . . . They had the disadvantage of not knowing reality. . . . So we come in, we've got some data. . . . Now we've got some responsibility, for the sake of history, to make goddam sure that these idiots don't prevail.

Vet 4: You know, it says here, "Disappointed by the world's unreasonableness, they see themselves condemned to ineffectiveness. They step aside in resignation and collapse before the stronger party." And I think that's where a lot of Vietnam veterans have made the mistake of resigning themselves to ineffectiveness. . . . No matter what we say, people aren't going to listen. We run for Congress and aren't going to be elected. You know, we have a presidential candidate right now who is a Vietnam veteran.[7]

Vet 3: Where's the power, then? Where is it coming from?

Vet 4: The power is coming from the Vietnam veterans [themselves], to get them out of that role of ineffectiveness [which is] that people aren't listening to them, that they don't have a say in what goes on in the world, and in society, and in relationship to everybody else. And it's getting those people who have resigned themselves to *un*resign themselves, to come back and say, hey, wait a minute, now. I *did* get something out of Vietnam, out of my experience. I am a different person, or even a better person. . . . I think it is the responsibility of those who have come out, or are coming out, to make others come out, too. And then we'll have the power. Then you can overcome that "stronger party" argument. . . .

Vet 1: . . . We faced a hostile environment here, one which we couldn't cope with. Our growing process [was arriving at] the awareness of the vulnerability even of strong men. . . . I was well disciplined. I was well trained. I was well schooled, and I had a lot of strong convictions. I am a strong man. And all of a sudden I find myself very weak, very vulnerable.—So we have to be aware that we need each other because we're vulnerable; then you become aware of the brotherhood, the bond that has to exist between us. And then you start to become much more aware—that, my God, the only thing I have is God. I mean, I've ended up with my whole family gone from me, kids, wife, the whole works. All of a sudden, everybody is against me. What—what is left? There's suicide, which was considered. Or is there a God? If there is no God then suicide is a hell of a good option. I don't want to preach, but that's where I come from. . . . Well, we got to work together or we're vulnerable. So we open up.

TOWARD A LATENT CHURCH

So they open up, though that alone does not provide the power to propel a nation from adolescence to adulthood. But the continuation of the veterans' exchange about Bonhoeffer's views on taking one's share of responsibility provides some interesting clues as to how this power can be generated. Vet 1, the officer who ran for Congress and has been working with refugees from Indochina, suddenly focuses on street people in Minneapolis, many of whom are Vietnam veterans:

Vet 1: You know, I've been with a couple of different groups of Vietnam veterans—in the city. . . . It's pretty hard to find a bond of love and concern and compassion any stronger anyplace in the world than I found in those groups. And I'm talking about guys who had nothing. I mean, most of the guys I was working with in the city came off the streets and they had nothing to go back to other than the streets. And they are concerned for one another. I mean, that's a pretty strong bond of brotherhood that says, hey, in all this . . . there is something pretty good about these guys. You know, it just . . . amazed me that I call them the street people, and it amazed me that they had so much compassion and concern for one another. And yet there were people, middle-class people, man, they would . . . on them. They'd say, these are scum. They wouldn't talk to them. But the bonding between them was something that, to me, was a . . . real awakening . . . because I realize that among the most discarded of our society there is an awful lot of strength. That I was never aware of before.

Vet 2: I've seen that too. But how are you going to get them to teach that to the rest of our society?
Vet 1: Well, maybe you don't have to. Maybe just a handful have become aware of it. Again, you talk about history. Not everybody changes history. But there are a few people who become aware of what's going on, and they have an impact on history. You know, we may not individually have an impact on history. But I think that as we do things as a total, it's going to be an impact on history.

What this man is describing is a prime example of one of the most striking phenomena observed by therapists working with Vietnam veterans: the warmth and spirituality, albeit of a rough kind, that prevails in their groups. What distinguishes them from the rest of a society not known for its long attention span is the patience and compassion their members have for one another. I was there when sixteen grown men, all of whom had serious problems themselves, listened for ninety minutes as one of their peers spoke about a suicide attempt. They encouraged him with soothing words. Those sitting next to him stroked his shoulders and hands. These groups are "a supportive, loving community and a surrogate for the friends he [the veteran] served with in Vietnam. In order to move beyond the war, to transcend its rage, guilt, and pain, the veteran must first remember, recount, confront, and reinterpret the painful incidents. This is an absolutely essential key to beginning the healing process."[8]

To Eberhard Bethge this augurs even more, namely, the dawn of the *sanctorum communio*, the communion of saints, in which Christ is present as community (see chapter 8). Although most veterans' groups may not have reached this stage, which requires faith and obedience, they clearly are what Paul Tillich calls a latent church; they have become "spiritual communities," distinct from the "manifest church" whose ultimate criterion is the faith and love of Christ. Tillich characterizes the "latent church" as consisting of groups who "show the power of the New Being in an impressive way":[9]

There are youth alliances, friendship groups, educational, artistic, and political movements, and, even more obviously, individuals without any visible relation to each other in whom the Spiritual Presence's impact is felt, although they are indifferent or hostile to all overt

51

expressions of religion. They do not belong to a church, but they are not excluded from the Spiritual Community. It is impossible to deny this if one looks at the manifold instances of profanization and demonization of the Spiritual Presence in those groups—the churches—which claim to be the Spiritual Community.[10]

The rap group listened intently as I read to them a statement by Tillich that has great import for Vietnam veterans:

> The ultimate criterion, the faith and love of the Christ, has not yet appeared to these groups. . . . As a consequence of their lack of this criterion, such groups are unable to actualize a radical self-negation and self-transformation as it is present as reality and symbol in the Cross of Christ. This means that they are . . . unconsciously driven toward the Christ, even though they reject him when he is brought to them through the preaching and actions of the Christian churches.[11]

The veterans listened quietly but did not comment. There are reasons why groups such as theirs tend to "reject Christ . . . when he is brought to them through preaching and actions." I will discuss reasons in the following chapter, on folly. To the veterans' ears, Bonhoeffer's assessment of the institutional church's performance rings painfully true:

> Our church, which has been fighting in these years only for its self-preservation, as though that were an end in itself, is incapable of taking the word of reconciliation and redemption to mankind and the world.[12]

4

Where America Failed Its Veterans

OF FOLLY

Folly is a more dangerous enemy to the good than evil. One can protest against evil; it can be unmasked and, if need be, prevented by force. Evil always carries the seeds of its own destruction, as it makes people, at the least, uncomfortable. Against folly we have no defence. Neither protest nor force can touch it; reasoning is no use; facts that contradict personal prejudices can simply be disbelieved—indeed, the fool can counter by criticizing them, and if they are undeniable, they can just be pushed aside as trivial exceptions. So the fool, as distinct from the scoundrel, is completely self-satisfied; in fact, he can easily become dangerous, as it does not take much to make him aggressive.[1]

Dietrich Bonhoeffer's thoughts on folly provide a much-needed opportunity for reflection on the host of follies committed during the Vietnam war and its aftermath. May I be forgiven for perhaps taking liberties with his ideas.

The saddest specimen of a fool dabbling in Vietnam-related matters—with the exception of the chaplains of the Veterans Administration—must surely be the institutional church. No effort has been made by any major denomination to fashion ministry to the special needs of a generation of men and women who feel let down by their God and their country in an unprecedented way. While it is true that valiant individuals such as William Mahedy in San Diego and Gary Berg in St. Cloud are thinking of ways to bring the Gospel back to these veterans who "flipped off" God in the steaming jungles of Indochina, neither the Roman Catholic church nor any major Protestant denomination seems to have grasped how important a resource these men and women could be for the Body of Christ. Mahedy writes, "Tragically, the Church has played as yet almost no role in assisting the vets to readjust back in the world. The religious and moral dimensions of their crisis have passed unnoticed by religious leaders, theologians, and the people in the pews."[2]

And yet, even if the extent of their pain seems meaningless to church bureaucracies, the sheer numbers of veterans should cause the churches to take notice. For if one includes the veterans' wives, lovers, children, and parents, the total of Americans suffering in one way or another from the war's aftermath might easily be twice as many as, for example, Episcopalians, Lutherans, and Congregationalists combined.

Not surprisingly, most veterans have little time for organized religion. In Vietnam they developed a deep dislike for military chaplains. This antipathy is in many cases unfair. I have often marveled at the immense courage and faith displayed by ministers in combat situations. Mahedy tells the story of a remarkable Lutheran pastor who in the siege of Khe Sanh in 1968 took the sacrament from soldier to soldier saying nothing but "the body of Christ." He quotes an eyewitness as saying, "With the smell of our dead buddies, stacked in empty bunkers, still in our noses, he walked among us with another broken body."

But the principal reason for the veterans' dislike of chaplains is none other than an ecclesial folly: Unlike their colleagues in most other armed forces, American military chaplains sport officers' rank insignia. They live in officers' quarters, eat in the officers' mess, and relax in the officers' club. To the soldiers fighting in Vietnam they were thus nothing but hated "lifers," no different from platoon leaders, company or battalion commanders, and "desk-top warriors." They were seen as public relations men for the commanding officers. The "sky pilots," as the troopers called the chaplains, were therefore men to whom the average "grunt" could not relate when in combat.

When the soldiers came home, they heard themselves denounced by ministers of the same denominations that had supplied chaplains to the armed forces. The Reverend Hayward Knight of the North Chicago VA reported, "One of my patients was actually told by the pastor of his home congregation from the pulpit to leave the church.

'We don't need your kind around here,' he said." Similarly, a member of one of my rap groups in Minnesota was told by a priest after Mass, "You have some nerve coming here." Of the fifteen veterans in another group, five left the church after hearing "goofy sermons" by the same priest, but on five different occasions. In every one of these homilies the soldiers fighting in Vietnam were accused of committing atrocities.

Smug and self-righteous religious liberals have caused much pain, writes Mahedy, who charges them with continuing to represent the worst of the antiwar movement of the sixties, with their inability to separate "the war from the warrior." Vietnam veteran John Fergueson, who is now an Episcopal priest, has provided two singularly shocking examples of clerical self-righteousness that he noted during a conference of clergy people. At one point, the participants were asked to say what they were experiencing during prayer. Fergueson writes,

> Men would speak out and receive reassuring words and often a hug or touch of support. In this deepened experience of prayer I was focused upon Vietnam. Suddenly a wave of love and peace swept over me. I was overcome and blurted out, "Thank you for forgiving me about Vietnam." There was silence and the sound of one or two people leaving the room. I had just uttered the ultimate obscenity. I had put God—forgiveness—and Vietnam together.[3]

In another incident, this former marine overheard two fellow ministers talking about him. One said to the other, "There goes the baby killer who thinks he is a priest."[4]

"One feels in fact, when talking to [a fool], that one is dealing, not with the man himself, but with slogans, catchwords, and the like," Bonhoeffer observes.[5] "I'm just totally overcome; that that's our country," said Vet 4, the farmer, when this passage was discussed in the Brainerd group. As the former soldiers tell it, the catchphrase "baby killer" had, at one point, become almost a synonym for Vietnam veteran. Hardly any of the nearly one hundred vets I worked with in Minnesota, either in rap groups or in individual counseling sessions, had *not* been called a baby killer within days of his return to the United States. One of them reported, "As I arrived at Milwaukee airport, there was a woman with two children. The kids wanted to approach me, but the mother pulled them back and said, 'Stay away from him, he's a baby killer.' "

Other veterans were physically attacked because their military haircuts and deep tans gave them away as Vietnam combatants. Veterans would pretend that they had been in Florida on vacation, or that they were stationed in Panama, just to avoid unpleasant arguments. Girls rejected their advances, saying, "I don't date baby killers." The foolish phrase "baby killer" caused serious damage to the relationships between the veterans and the opposite sex. Patients in the St. Cloud VA estimated that up to 70 percent of the soldiers in their units had received "Dear John" letters from their girlfriends or wives. Often the key phrase in those letters was that the women wished no further contacts with a "baby killer."

Anyone familiar with combat situations can easily imagine the devastating effect of such correspondence: After weeks in the jungle the trooper returns to base camp. Tired, numbed, and still in sweaty, filthy fatigues, he goes to mail call, which is the highlight in the day of any military unit, especially in a wartime situation. He receives his wad of mail, flips through it, recognizes his girlfriend's handwriting, and saves this letter for last. He will open it when he is showered and stretched out on his bunk. And then he finds out that it is all over between him and her. "I have seen more than one suicide precipitated by such an event," writes Stephen Howard, who is both a psychiatrist and a Vietnam combat veteran.[6]

But "Dear John" letters did not result only in suicides, as Emanuel Tanay, a psychiatrist, reports:

> In January of 1969 I went to Vietnam . . . to testify at a general court martial of a U.S. marine charged with four counts of murder. This twenty-year-old young man had a history of being an outstanding, well disciplined soldier, performing his duties with distinction. In May of 1968 he developed a high fever and was evacuated from the combat area to a hospital. . . . On the day he was discharged from the hospital . . . he received a letter from his girlfriend . . . informing him that she was getting married. Two days later he killed four Vietnamese whom he considered Viet Cong suspects. The extensive evaluations of this young soldier established clearly that the rage precipitated by the "Dear John" letter was the causative factor in the homicides. The military attorneys with whom I worked expressed the view that the frequency *and hostility* [my italics] of the so-called "Dear John" letters was never

so high as during the Vietnam war. They showed me numerous letters
. . . some of [which] were accompanied by pictures vividly illustrating
the written word. There was even a tape recording sent in by a
girl . . . ; [it] recorded an amorous session with the new boyfriend for
the benefit of the old boyfriend.[7]

If we admit that despair is the prevalent condition among Vietnam
veterans, it must surely be seen in the context of what Bonhoeffer
observed about folly, namely, that we have no defense against it. It
might well be argued that hardly any living group of Americans has
been exposed to as massive a concentration of folly as have these
men: There was, at first, the folly of a government that didn't even
know whom it was fighting in Vietnam. Until the mid-1960s Secre-
tary of State Dean Rusk thought that China was the real enemy.
"Liberals" on the other hand saw in Ho Chi Minh a benign agrarian
reformer. Both sides disregarded the overwhelming evidence that
since 1923 Ho had been a Soviet Comintern agent whose initial
revolutionary act was the betrayal of prominent Vietnamese na-
tionalists to the French Sureté so as to eliminate these democratic
competitors.[8]

The next folly was to commit young draftees to a war without
telling them what they were risking their lives for. Very few of the
veterans I have worked with in Minnesota were familiar with the
historical, political, sociological, and cultural background of the
conflict. Then there was the folly of making these soldiers fight
"with the right arm chained behind the back to the left foot," as they
used to say when they were prevented from pursuing the enemy to
his sanctuaries in "neutral" Laos and Cambodia, and in North
Vietnam; furthermore, the standard procedure of abandoning territory almost immediately after it had been wrested from the foe was
foolish by any military and indeed logical measure. What happened
daily in hundreds of operations throughout South Vietnam ultimately proved true in a folly of global importance when strategically vital bases, which had cost the American taxpayers billions of
dollars, were to all intents and purposes given to the Russians. These
bases are now posing a threat even to U.S. territory.[9]

There was the folly of not declaring war, a folly that resulted in the
first unlimited media coverage of any major armed conflict in this
century. In every democratic society, a declaration of war automat-

ically results in a temporary restriction of the freedom of the press for the sake of national security and the protection of human lives. Thus, in all previous wars American media reports were censored. Britain did the same during the Falklands crisis. In the case of Vietnam, the absence of censorship put our own side at an unfair disadvantage and aided and abetted the psychological warfare of the adversary. It brought the ugliness of war home to the living rooms of a smug civilian population—but primarily the ugliness of the war that was fought by the U.S. and its allies, and rarely the ugliness of the enemy's behavior.[10]

This in turn led to the foolish way in which civilians turned on their own young men as they came back from the war. "[The veterans'] peers, especially those higher on the ladder of education and wealth, shunned them. Vets were considered moral outcasts, baby killers, perpetrators of atrocities. One did not associate with such people and retain one's own sense of self-worth. The message from these guardians of America's conscience was clear: Vietnam veterans were pariahs. They were immoral and evil people. To their own peer groups, those with whom they had grown up, with whom they shared the same Little League games, rock music, sexual adventures, they had become non-persons."[11]

According to Myra MacPherson, "The obtuseness, the downright stupidity in the way troubled veterans were treated a decade ago, is one of the greatest indictments of our society."[12] Returning soldiers were spat on by strangers. They were yelled at, "Welcome home, asshole."[13] Lenny Roberts, now the maintenance foreman of the Lutheran School of Theology at Chicago, had human feces thrown at him after his release from the Great Lakes Naval Hospital where he was treated for war wounds that had almost killed him.[14] Timothy C. Sims, a Marine Corps veteran who is now a Lutheran chaplain in the U.S. Navy, writes, "Alexander Solzhenitsyn taught us what a gulag was. Gulags are Russian forced labor camps. But there are other kinds of gulags besides the state-run institutions. Gulags can also be unspoken societal conspiracies to overlook, avoid, ignore. During college, I entered the gulag of the ignored Vietnam vet."[15]

One ex-marine in my Brainerd group told us what happened to him when he tried to enroll at Berkeley: "I was physically attacked by eight students, including co-eds. I flattened them all, ran out of the building and hailed a cab. At first, the driver said he did not transport 'baby killers.' I just put my hand around his throat, and he took me where I wanted to go."

Bonhoeffer's words, "The power of some needs the folly of others," particularly appealed to the Brainerd group:

Vet 3: . . . An example [for this is] Jane Fonda. She was their [the North Vietnamese's] power, but she was her own folly. They used her for their own needs when she went over there, you know, and played the—

Vet 4: That's because she was stupid, too. . . .

Vet 1: Folly . . . When I saw that, she was the first person I thought of. You know, they got . . . power from her folly. It's that simple. She went over there ignorant and did more damage than she did any good.

Vet 2: She did a lot of damage to a lot of veterans, too, now. And it made them feel like—

It should be borne in mind that this discussion took place shortly after the twentieth anniversary of the Tet offensive, which was commemorated by scores of television programs. They showed, among others, film clips of Jane Fonda's visit to Hanoi. Especially galling to the veterans was one scene in which the actress mockingly aimed a North Vietnamese anti-aircraft gun at imaginary U.S. bombers. Fonda's recent apologies for her behavior are seen by many veterans as an insincere and self-serving maneuver. A bumper sticker declaring Vietnam Veterans Are Not Fonda Jane is their reply to her acts of folly. It is interesting to note, though, why their wrath focuses on Jane Fonda but spares Joan Baez, who had been equally vociferous in her opposition to the war in Vietnam. "Joan Baez has voiced second thoughts about the role she played in those days, and that's why we are no longer angry with her," one veteran explained. "But Jane Fonda is what Bonhoeffer would call 'a stubborn fool.'" The others nodded.

CONTEMPT FOR HUMANITY?

There is a very real danger of our drifting into an attitude of contempt for humanity. We know quite well that we have no right to do so, and that it

would lead us into the most sterile relation to our fellow-man. . . . God himself did not despise humanity, but became man for men's sake.[16]

When the Brainerd group came to this passage, one of the most telling exchanges ensued. They ignored the part about God's becoming man for men's sake. But they also made it clear that their long suffering had taken most of them beyond the stage of contempt for their fellow men.

At this point in the discussion Vet 2, the graduate student of psychology, deliberately took a provocative line. "I wanted to jazz it up a little, to bring in some more tension," he told me later. In addition to the group of five quoted so far, a sixth man was involved. He had spent his year in Vietnam sweeping mines along the same stretch of road. Now he works as a therapist at the VA.

The discussion began with a contemptuous remark by Vet 2 about contemporaries who were not in Vietnam.

Vet 1: I don't like your attitude. What makes us any better than anybody else other than the fact that we've got more responsibility because we have more experience than they have?

Vet 2: Well, we didn't run to Canada. We didn't . . . get school deferments. We didn't hide there. We did what we thought was right.

Vet 1: We can't live our lives based upon being angry at them. . . . What have they gained?

Vet 3: Gentlemen, I thought I was an equal. Why should I give somebody like that—

Vet 1: Not equal. They are not equal. None of us are really equal. . . . There are some areas in which you can excel over me intellectually—and some areas where I excel. But we all have the responsibility for excelling in those areas where we have some sense of direction.

Vet 3: But, Uwe, do you think that we did drift into a bit of contempt for humanity?

Siemon-Netto: Certainly at some stage in their post-Vietnam experience vets were drifting into it. I don't know how far it went. But it's something you have to watch.

Vet 6: How much energy does that consume? . . . How much energy do I put into being contemptuous toward someone else, for being pissed off all the time about something that happened twenty years ago? . . . For being pissed off at the person who went to Canada or the person who went to Sweden or the person who ended up in school? . . . You see, I'm not there any longer.

Siemon-Netto: No, I know that.

Vet 6: I have found that that burns way too much energy. I refuse to allow Vietnam to dictate my life, and I refuse to allow myself, you know, to be pissed off at somebody who had gone to Canada. Because I feel they've got their own hell to live with also, and I allow them to live their hell and I'm going to get on with my life.

Vet 2: I don't see where contempt has to be time-consuming. You just don't give a damn about them—and if you don't give a damn about them you're not going to waste a whole lot of time thinking about them. The only time you're going to get pissed off is if somebody brings it up. . . . Well, we can think about this all day long. It's there.

Vet 1: But where will contempt get you? The biggest problem, the weakness I have is that when I get upset, [feel] contempt, anger, I want to . . . hide. To screw the world.—But what's the end result? Nothing! So I kind of venture out into the world and end up going back and hiding. I put my pack on and go home. And I'll stay out there.

Vet 5: It's useless, the contempt. . . . What are you so pissed off at? Does it really bother you if that guy went to Canada or that guy got a school deferment or whatever?

Vet 3: Yeah, it does bother me. It . . . bothers me a lot because them sons of bitches don't have the problem that we've got. They have got good jobs. They got . . . families. They got homes. They got it . . . made. That's what bothers me.

Vet 5: Some do, some don't, just like we—

Vet 2: Well, a lot more of them do than we do.

Vet 5: Well, they made their choice. You made your choice to go [to Vietnam]. I mean, nobody . . . forced you to go. Let's face it.

Vet 2: So why should they have it better than us? They don't have problems—

Vet 5: Well, we don't know that—

5

Good from Evil

A FEW ARTICLES OF FAITH ON
THE SOVEREIGNTY OF GOD
IN HISTORY[1]

I believe that God will bring good out of evil, even out of the greatest evil. For this purpose he needs men who make the best use of everything. I believe that God will give us all the strength we need to help us to resist in times of distress. But he never gives it in advance, lest we should rely on ourselves and not on him alone. A faith such as this should allay all our fears for the future. I believe that even our mistakes and shortcomings are turned to good account, and that it is no harder for God to deal with them than with our supposedly good deeds. I believe that God is no timeless fate, but that he waits for and answers sincere prayers and responsible actions.[2]

In the summer of 1987 I spent a day with Vet 1, the officer; he had once attended a Roman Catholic seminary and left it just weeks before ordination. I had met him twenty-two years earlier under less than cordial circumstances in central Vietnam. Convinced that I was an East German spy, he refused to let me into the camp of a U.S. advisory team of which he was the senior officer. It was by chance that we ran into each other again in Brainerd; now we became friends.

Vet 1 is a highly educated man and a devout Christian whose faith had not become one of the casualties of the Vietnam war. As we walked around his property in central Minnesota where he is raising ducks, he attributed both the disaster in Vietnam and the lamentable treatment of the veterans to "the lack of a sense of history" among most Americans. "Things would have turned out differently had our leaders and people been informed about the background of the conflict, about historical precedents, and parallels," he said, adding, "If you have no sense of history, you have no sense of destiny, and having no sense of destiny is a luxury veterans cannot afford."

As I worked with the veterans in Minnesota, I discovered that, next to a deplorably low level of catechetical instruction, a lack of historical knowledge had most aggravated their *spiritual* crisis. But I also discovered that they were much more eager for historical information than the average American. My three rap groups asked me for a discourse on the historical background of the Vietnam war, and the Veterans Administration in St. Cloud organized two lectures on the same subject; they were well attended. Veterans said that they were hungry for historical information.

Any meaningful ministry to this group of men must place a heavy emphasis on history if they are to develop, in the words of Vet 1, "a sense of destiny," the absence of which renders them incapable of guiding their nation to its destiny. Bonhoeffer's insights will prove very helpful in a situation where sufferers are trying to find out if their pain was at least worthwhile.

That good comes out of evil is of course not just biblical wisdom, though the salvation of humanity as a consequence of history's most heinous crime, the murder of God's Son, is the best example for the truth of this claim. But the history of the Christian era is a succession of evil deeds with astonishingly beneficial results.

The Hellenization of the ancient Mediterranean world was clearly accomplished with violence; but ultimately it also assured the success of the Gospel, as Kurt Dietrich Schmidt points out.[3] The Roman conquest of what now is Germany, Britain, and France surely caused a great deal of suffering, but without it there would not have been a Western civilization with all its advances in the arts, the sciences, and philosophy. If colonialism was an evil, it nevertheless led to the creation and development of the United States of America.

"I believe God can and will bring good . . . even out of the greatest evil," writes Bonhoeffer. One of the greatest evils to plague the world was the Nazi regime that killed Bonhoeffer and millions of others. But, as Bonhoeffer observes, "It is one of the most surprising experiences, but at the same time one of the most incontrovertible, that evil—often in a surprisingly short time—proves its own folly and defeats its own object."[4] The evil of World War II nevertheless advanced the rebirth of the Jewish nation. To be sure, this caused new suffering, this time among the Palestinians. But if history is any guide we may fairly assume that God will bring good out of this evil as well.

Dietrich Bonhoeffer's words proved especially prophetic where his own country was concerned. When the war that cost him his life was over, there emerged at least in the western half of Germany a democratic, stable, and caring form of government. More astonishingly still, centuries of Franco-German hostility vanished to the extent that opinion polls in both nations indicate that they regard each other as friends. This was accomplished not only by the wisdom of ardently Christian leaders such as Charles de Gaulle and Konrad Adenauer but by the suffering of humble men. It is now generally acknowledged that the Germans and French owe the harmony that exists between them to a considerable extent to the favorable reports of returning prisoners of war about the way they were treated by "enemy" civilians.[5]

Even where evil does take a little longer to "defeat its own object," to use Bonhoeffer's words, the good that will come out of it is often clearly discernible well ahead of time. The communist subjugation of half of Europe is a case in point. It is in East Germany, Poland, and the Soviet Union itself that the Christian faith is experiencing its most important renewal, which is already affecting the West as well.

Vietnam veterans struggling with the "AWOL God" need to hear the historical truth that so far, not Christian faith but its evil competitor, ideology, has always proved short-lived. According to Bonhoeffer, "Ideologies vent their furies on man and then leave him as a bad dream leaves the waking dreamer. The memory of them is bitter. They have not made the man stronger or more mature; they have made him poorer and more distrustful. In the hour of this unhappy awakening, if God reveals Himself to men as the Creator before whom man can live only as the creature, that is grace and the blessing of poverty."[6]

As we shall see in chapter 7, on suffering, the lack of historical information and religious instruction have deprived the veterans of the comforting news that they, the rejected, are sharing the fate of the ultimate victim of human rejection—God. They overlook the fact that all rejected beings share the same foes. One is cowardice (chapter 3), another is folly (chapter 4). Ideology is a third, as Bonhoeffer points out above. And he names several others that have become painfully familiar to the veterans—among them radicalism and compromise: "Radicalism hates time, and compromise hates eternity. Radicalism hates patience, and compromise hates decision. Radicalism hates wisdom, and compromise hates simplicity. Radicalism hates moderation and measure, and compromise hates the immeasurable. Radicalism hates the real, and compromise hates the word."[7]

To the veterans, this is the most accurate description of one particular aspect of their experience. But it does not answer their key question, raised by historical facts Mahedy describes thus:

> The biblical God remains a God of mystery, not of manageability. In Vietnam, God could not be persuaded to stop the Vietcong atrocities against the Vietnamese or their relentless killing of American soldiers. The North Vietnamese Army, despite the fact that they were an arm of an explicitly atheistic system of government, continued to pour into South Vietnam, inflicting heavy losses on our own people. We couldn't get a handle on God to have him halt the influx of the "heathen horde." Much more to the point, God did nothing to slow the descent of American troops into the barbarism and brutality of war. He allowed men who believed in him to taste fully the savagery of killing. Evil is, on some levels, almost a transcendent reality, far more, apparently, than the sum of all its parts. Evil on this scale becomes unmanageable, itself a mystery that can be neither explained nor articulated. God allowed teenaged soldiers . . . to live out the story of the book of Genesis. They ate of the tree of the knowledge of good and evil. As a consequence, they were expelled from the garden of innocence. For most Americans, the story is a platitude; for vets it is a personal experience. The real question is not why it happened, but why it happens at all.[8]

I do not pretend here to comprehensively study the question of theodicy. This book is, after all, an attempt to make some theological and historical sense of the suffering of one generation of American men; it is not a definitive study of why there is evil in the world. But among the many theodicies there is one that makes the most sense to me, a former war correspondent.

Having experienced much evil as a child and adolescent in Germany, and, later, during my thirty-two years as a journalist, I am left with two options: Either I become a cynic, rejecting God altogether or seeing God as a less than perfect deity, or I adopt a line of argument that was first presented by St. Augustine and recently named by theologian Stephen T. Davis who writes,

> Obviously, in making humans free God ran the risk that they would choose evil rather than good. The possibility of freely doing evil is the inevitable companion of the possibility of freely doing good. Unfortunately, this is not what human beings did; they chose to go wrong; they fell into sin. So God is not to be blamed for the existence of evil in the world—we are. Of course, God is *indirectly* responsible for evil in the sense that he created the conditions given which evil would come into existence (i.e., he gave us free choice), and he foreknew the evil choices we would make. But even given these conditions, it was not inevitable that evil exist. . . . Humans could have chosen to obey God. Sadly, they didn't. Why then did God create free moral agents in the first place? Does it not look as if his plan went wrong. . . ? Not so, says the Free Will Doctrine. God's policy decision to make us free was wise, for it will turn out better in the long run that we act freely, even if we sometimes err, than it would have turned out had we been created innocent automata, programmed always to do the good. God's decision will turn out to be wise because the good that will in the end result from his decision will outweigh the evil that will in the end result from it. In the *eschaton* it will be seen that God chose the best course and that the favorable balance of good and evil that will exist then was obtainable by God in no other way.[9]

This is, of course, what Paul Tillich means when he writes, "One of Martin Luther's most profound insights was that God made himself small for us in Christ. In so doing, he left us our freedom and our humanity."[10] It parallels what Douglas John Hall says about suffering: "It is true, of course, that God 'allows' suffering, because God 'allows human sin;' it is the consequence of God's not only allowing but willing human freedom. Yet allowing something is not *intending* it. To take the best illustration of all, the cross of Christ, it could not be claimed . . . that God intended his Son to be crucified, yet God did quite obviously allow it."[11]

This is the kind of theology that in my experience made sense to the Vietnam veterans I counseled both privately and in rap groups.

Bonhoeffer's emphasis on the contrast between the "immanent righteousness of history [that] rewards and punishes only men's deeds," and "the eternal righteousness of God [that] tries and judges their hearts" strikes me as an important tool for intelligent spiritual care for the Vietnam veterans.[12]

For only if they can bridge the perceived gap between historical phenomena and the notion of a good, almighty, and loving God will they see the futility of cynicism and despair. Only then will they see any reason to accomplish their task of guiding their nation from adolescence to maturity.

6

Making Sense of the Veterans' Pain

SYMPATHY AND SUFFERING

Christ kept himself from suffering till his hour had come, but when it did come he met it as a free man, seized it, and mastered it. Christ, so the scriptures tell us, bore the sufferings of all humanity in his own body as if they were his own—a thought beyond our comprehension—accepting them of his own free will. We are certainly not Christ; we are not called on to redeem the world by our own deeds and sufferings, and we need not try to assume such an impossible burden. We are not lords, but instruments in the hand of the Lord of history; and we can share in other people's suffering only to a very limited degree. We are not Christ, but if we want to be Christians, we must have some share in Christ's large-heartedness by acting with responsibility and in freedom when the hour of danger comes, and by showing a real sympathy that springs, not from fear, but from the liberating and redeeming love of Christ for all who suffer. Mere waiting and looking on is not Christian behaviour. The Christian is called to sympathy and action, not in the first place by his own sufferings, but by the sufferings of his brethren for whose sake Christ suffered.[1]

Making sense of suffering is nowhere more difficult than in a prosperous society. I believe that a significant reason for our ignoble treatment of the Vietnam veterans is that in the United States suffering often seems to be a fashionable exercise of the basically comfortable and is therefore not recognized or countenanced where and when it seriously occurs.

Dean W. Bard has remarked upon a conference he attended, at which a small but ardent group of preachers and panelists "shared" the many sides of the existential pain which they were experiencing.

And the pain was taken seriously by most of the conferees. Before long, everyone seemed to be in pain. In the middle of this contagious unhappiness, Bard ran into a visiting professor and asked about his general health and well-being. "How are you?" he asked. "Well," the professor said, "I'm in pain. I guess it's the thing to be in."[2]

There are, no doubt, also some Vietnam veterans among those to whom Bard's further observations apply:

> We may define our relationship with other people on the basis of our victim status. But the distortions and the unhappiness which can follow are undermining, debilitating, and demoralizing. If we fall into that bottomless pit, we can easily become more than victims—we may emerge as losers. . . . A passive dependence replaces the kind of active self-giving which is exemplified in the mission of Jesus Christ.[3]

But if the veterans' sufferings are to have any beneficial results at all, these men cannot afford to wallow in them. This was clearly understood by the veterans I was working with in Minnesota. As the Brainerd group discussed Bonhoeffer's essay, Vet 5, the builder, made the poignant remark,

> I think one thing needs to be pointed out—and that is the combat veterans' great capacity for suffering. They have experienced so much suffering that it became common for them not to grieve and . . . just bury [the pain] inside themselves. . . . The negative thing they carried back with them to society was to just let the suffering pile on because [they felt], hey, I can handle this. I can take it. I took it in 'Nam, I can take it now.

But whether one suffers bravely, whether one wants to "master the pain," as another group member said, or whether one wishes for the pain to simply go away, as a third veteran blurted out, none of the above will happen or be effective until the meaning of human sin is grasped. For the veterans' spiritual darkness is really "an overpowering awareness of the extent of human sin."[4] On the one hand, they experienced the sin of war which, in Mahedy's words, is "the ultimate failure of humankind to reach the God-given objectives of maintaining love and justice in our relationships with each other and making a final turn to God." On the other hand, the veterans' own reaction was precisely what the authors of the Augsburg Confession described as "the more serious faults of human nature": "ignoring God, despising him, lacking fear and trust in him, hating his judgment and fleeing it, being angry at him, despairing of his grace."[5]

Though my concern here is the impact the veterans may have on the future of American society, the above passage from the Book of Concord invites reflection on appropriate spiritual care for them. For their dilemma, as evidenced by flashbacks, nightmares, a sense of numbing, and a feeling of alienation, stands as a paradigm for the human condition.

Dr. Arthur Kuhne, who has worked extensively in the area of post-traumatic stress disorder, considers "the resolution of the patients' spiritual problems the most important aspect of the healing process."[6] Mahedy makes the same point: "Therapy may reduce some clinical symptoms, but it does not resolve the ache in the deepest regions of the soul."[7] Once again, Dietrich Bonhoeffer, a psychiatrist's son, provides a helpful insight as to why this should be so: "No psychology knows that people perish through sin and are saved only through the cross of Christ."[8] Mahedy agrees: "Sin is, of course, largely denied by our therapeutic culture."[9]

But close cooperation between psychologist and theologian is possible. Unfortunately, the veterans' distrust of most clergymen—their misogyny precludes a role for women in this endeavor—complicates the task. While I have encountered highly dedicated VA chaplains, their frequent lack of combat experience makes this acceptance by the veterans difficult. I was accepted not because of my theological training but because to them I was a "fellow vet" who, though not a soldier, had shared their fear, horror, and despair.

Ideally, ministers to this sizable community should be recruited from among the three million men who have served in Vietnam; time and again group members have told me that their confidence is limited to people who have shared their experience. Except for some charismatic groups, however, none of the major churches has, to my knowledge, made any effort in this direction. Yet excellent candidates can be found, especially among former medics, many of whom are among the most caring, loving, intelligent, brave, and spiritual men I have encountered in my three decades as a journalist. I have found that these qualities survived even alcoholism, drug addiction, anger, and disillusionment. Whenever a member of one of my rap groups went "into a tailspin," ex-medics would softly stroke him, talk to him soothingly, comfort him the way they comforted wounded and dying men in combat. Bonhoeffer's words, "The Christian is called to sympathy and action, not in the first place by his own sufferings, but by the sufferings of his brethren," seem an apt description of the attitude of these remarkable men.

Minister and psychologist can and should jointly develop a potent program to help the veterans resolve their spiritual problems. This was clarified for me by Robert Bertram, systematic theologian and psychotherapist, who pointed out that according to Article II of the Augsburg Confession humans are "unable by nature to have true fear of God and true faith in God." He suggested that therapists retarget the veterans' anxieties "to the only one worth fearing, namely the God they cannot fear by nature." And then the Gospel would liberate them from being afraid. This is presumably what Mahedy means when he writes,

> Vets . . . whose neat notions of God, self, and the world have been shattered by evil of great magnitude have been thrust unwillingly into the same condition of spiritual darkness that mystics know is the prerequisite for the deepest knowledge of God possible in this life. The first voluntary step in the journey out of the night is to cease the frantic efforts to escape from the darkness, realizing that one already has begun to grasp God in a very different way—this is true even though one wants nothing further to do with God. The painful and haunting presence of God, even among vets who have attempted for years to dismiss him, is a fair indication of God's tenacity. The poet Francis Thompson likened God to a hound who pursues a person "down the nights and down the days." Escape and evasion tactics—at which the vets are experts—do not work against God. One must first stop running in the darkness and allow the "hound of heaven" to catch his quarry. In practical terms this means, first of all, that the "God question" must be pursued openly rather than left to simmer on the back burner of the mind. For those who wish to face the issue in the context of the Christian faith, the focus—even though in anger—must be directly on God.[10]

The questions are, then, how to pursue the God question openly and how the veterans are to arrive at a state Mahedy describes as follows:

> After having jettisoned the easy god of American mythology in favor of

the One who can be known only in a cloud of unknowing and then having striven to banish hatred from the soul, living according to a deeper kind of love, a person may become aware that a final act of faith is necessary. This act of faith requires that one place oneself, one's family, friends and enemies, the world and all its gulags in the hands of God. The angry challenge hurled at God by vets and others who demand His presence in a malignant world is finally countered by a challenge from God. The challenge is simply to call Him "Father," as Jesus did.[11]

I have found that this can only be accomplished by a theology of the suffering God, a theology that makes sense to the veterans. To develop it we must first return to Tillich's concept of Sin, or estrangement. Tillich describes unbelief not as a denial of God but as a "disruption of man's cognitive participation in God."[12] Where the Vietnam veterans are concerned, Tillich's coupling of the terms "unbelief" and "un-love" is of relevance. Having established humanity's unbelief and estrangement from God as the center of humankind's being, Tillich concludes that this is "ultimately identical with un-love; both point to man's estrangement from God."[13]

One of the most dramatic aspects of the pain suffered by many veterans is that with them the manifestation of unlove seems almost total. Augustine's dictum, "Sin is love which desires finite goods for their own sake and not for the sake of the ultimate good," does not apply to them because the numbing effect of the Vietnam war and its aftermath often precludes even the kind of love that fits this description. Tillich's insight that "love of one's self and one's world is distorted if it does not penetrate through the finite to its infinite ground" does not apply either because very often even that kind of self-love and love of the world is missing or at least dormant.

Yet it is the relative absence of this distorted kind of self-love that points to fascinating opportunities. As I have observed both in rap sessions and while counseling individual veterans, these men are yearning for some contact with God. This gives special significance to Tillich's words that "grace, as the infusion of love, is the power which overcomes estrangement." As we shall see in the next chapter, grace brings forgiveness, which is the principal feature of Bonhoeffer's concept of the *sanctorum communio*, ending estrangement and bringing reunion.

If it is true, as I have stated above, that the Vietnam veterans in their estrangement from God stand as a paradigm for the human condition, then we must ponder their plight in the only way their condition can be approached—christologically. Ironically, it may prove helpful that they have "flipped off" the God in whom they still believe. They are not likely to reach out for God. They are far too angry with God to "seek him in [their] distress" (Hosea 5:15). Thus, they are irreligious, as Bonhoeffer would define the term.

To Bonhoeffer, religion is the futile search for the direct way to God. It is part of human nature. It is what Augustine called the restlessness in man's heart. It is what Gerhard O. Forde finds wrong with three principal atonement theories: Anselm's doctrine of vicarious satisfaction, Abelard's moral influence theory and all its variants, and Gustaf Aulen's idea of a victory over tyrants.[14] Forde comments: "The aim [of these views] is to escape, to ascend toward God, whether by law and moral improvement or by victory over the tyrants who claim us to our mortality and finitude."[15]

Clearly, this kind of religiosity would be meaningless to the veterans in their state of estrangement, and Bonhoeffer would probably agree with them. He sees in religion and morality "the greatest danger for the recognition of divine grace"[16] and says religion belongs to the flesh of man. His answer to this impasse is as follows:

> For there is another way; it is God's way to man, the way of revelation and grace, the way of the Christ, the way of justification by grace alone. Not we go to God, but God comes to us. Not religion makes us good before God, but God alone makes us good. But that means: the way to God is once and for all hopeless where God does not come to us; it means that our religion is nothing if God does not say 'yes' to it. Not religion, but revelation, not the way to God, but God's way to man: That is the meaning of Christianity.[17]

And:

> Not our religion—not even the Christian religion!—But God's grace: that is the message of . . . all of Christianity.[18]

PARTICIPATING IN GOD'S SUFFERING

The question that then arises is how can the Vietnam veterans be persuaded to open themselves to that way of God, whom they perceive as having turned against them? Veterans have wept when told, often for the first time in their lives, that the very essence of the Gospel is that God was suffering with them. The God whom they thought of as having gone AWOL in Vietnam turned out to be with them all the way to their cry of God's dereliction. Mahedy writes,

> No Christian image is more subversive or troublesome than the cross. When Jesus confronted evil, He lost. When He faced sin, it overcame Him. Though He desired to be spared suffering, He was not. Like all of us, He protested the approach of death, but even He yielded before it. . . . The worst of it is that Jesus, too, underwent not just the physical agony of crucifixion but spiritual anguish as well. The primordial "dark night" experience was His. When death approached, Jesus cried out, making His own the words of the psalmist, "My God, my God, why have you forsaken me?" (Mark 15:34)[19]

What Mahedy, an Episcopalian and former Augustinian monk, is pointing to is a traditionally Lutheran insight. In Forde's words, "The cry of dereliction from the cross is real. One cannot, for Luther, look on the cross as though it were simply the apex of life of high moral purpose in which Jesus now remains true to the end and actively offers himself to God on our behalf. That would fit the picture of the heavenward traffic but not Luther's reversal of direction. [To Luther] Christ feels himself in his conscience to be cursed by God and really and truly enters into eternal damnation from God the Father for us."[20]

Jürgen Moltmann calls this forsakenness and rejection by the Father "the suffering within the suffering of Jesus." He explains, "God does not become a religion so that one participates in him with the appropriate religious thoughts and feelings. God does not become the law, so that one participates in him through obedience to the law. God does not become an ideal so that one may enter communion with him through steadily striving effort. God humbles himself and takes upon himself the eternal death of the godless and the godforsaken, so that the godless and the godforsaken may experience communion with him."[21]

What may be termed Luther's formula of divine vaccination against pain and death, *mors contra mortem et dolor contra dolorem* [death against death and pain against pain] has thus a special meaning to the Vietnam veterans once the "happy exchange" is explained to them in the way Forde does:

> The question of Luther's doctrine of atonement is . . . how God can succeed in giving himself to us so as actually to take away our sin, to destroy the barrier between us and God. This is the reason for the prominence in Luther's thought of "the happy exchange." Christ, through his actual coming, his cross and resurrection, takes away our sinful and lost nature and gives us his sinless and righteous nature. This cannot be an abstract metaphysical transaction. We must, through the cross of Christ, his terrible suffering and death, be actually purchased, won, indeed killed and made alive. If it is to be a "happy exchange", our hearts must be captured by it.[22]

The proper approach to spiritual care for Vietnam veterans is therefore to stress God's pain, which to Kazoh Kitamori, a Japanese proponent of the theology of the cross, is, "in concrete terms, the forgiveness of Sin,"[23] and the very foundation of God's love.[24] Kitamori writes, "God's pain gives man's pain its meaning and value. . . . What gives human pain its value is God's pain as transcendent grace. We recognize that of all the spiritual experiences of man suffering is the most valuable and the deepest."[25]

Here, then, lies the answer to the question Vietnam veterans have asked time and again, ever since their return from a war that by its very nature was sin, to their own country which rejected them: "How can we make sense of our suffering?"

The answer is: God suffers to end our sinful estrangement from God. And as we have now become part of God, we bear our own suffering as what Bonhoeffer calls "the badge of true discipleship"[26] and as what to Luther was "one of the marks of the true church."[27] "In the words of K. F. Hartmann's poem, 'it is in suffering that the Master imprints upon our minds and hearts his own all-valid image.' "[28] The suffering will still be painful, but it now has the meaning whose absence made it unbearable to the veterans. Bonhoeffer elaborates,

> Just as Christ is Christ only in virtue of his suffering and rejection, so the disciple is disciple only insofar as he shares his Lord's suffering and rejection and crucifixion. Discipleship means adherence to the person of Jesus, and therefore submission to the law of Christ which is the law of the cross.[29]

To endure the cross, Bonhoeffer says, "is not a tragedy; it is the suffering which is the fruit of exclusive allegiance to Jesus Christ. . . , an essential part of the specifically Christian life."[30] In a passage singularly pertinent to the suffering veterans Bonhoeffer states,

> Jesus says that every Christian has his own cross waiting for him, a cross destined and appointed by God. Each must endure his allotted share of suffering and rejection. But each has a different share: some God deems worthy of the highest form of suffering, and gives them the grace of martyrdom, while others he does not allow to be tempted above that which they are able to bear. But it is the one and the same cross in every case.[31]

To this I add two observations by Moltmann, both of which are applicable to the veterans' predicament. The first is that "the godforsaken and the rejected can accept himself where he recognizes the crucified God who has already accepted him."[32] It would therefore be an absurdity to "flip off" God. By flipping off the God of Christianity, the veteran achieves the opposite of what he is yearning for; as he rejects God's solidarity he rejects his own acceptance by God. Moltmann's second observation points to what might be called God's assignment to sufferers such as the Vietnam veterans: "Having died in Christ and been resurrected to a new life, as Paul says in Rom. 6:8, the believer participates in real terms in God's suffering in the world, because he participates . . . in God's love. On the other hand, he participates in the concrete suffering of the world, because he has made it his own suffering in the cross of Christ."[33]

This refers of course to what may well be termed Bonhoeffer's most profound insight, to which I referred in chapter 1:

> Christians range themselves with God in his suffering. That is what distinguishes them from the heathen. As Jesus asked in Gethsemane, "Could ye not watch with me one hour?" That is the exact opposite of what the religious man expects from God. Man is challenged to participate in the sufferings of God in a godless world.[34]

7

A World Come of Age

PRESENT AND FUTURE

The force of circumstances has brought us into a situation where we have to give up being "anxious about tomorrow" (Matt. 6:34). But it makes all the difference whether we accept this willingly and in faith (as the Sermon on the Mount intends), or under continual constraint. For most people, the compulsory abandonment of planning for the future means that they are forced back into living just for the moment, irresponsibly, frivolously or resignedly; some few dream longingly of better times to come, and try to forget the present. We find both these courses equally impossible, and there remains for us only the very narrow way . . . of living every day as if it were our last, and yet living in faith and responsibility as though there were to be a great future: "Houses and fields and vineyards shall again be bought in this land," proclaims Jeremiah (32:15), in paradoxical contrast to his prophecies of woe, just before the destruction of the holy city. It is a sign from God and a pledge of a fresh start and a great future, just when all seems black. Thinking and acting for the sake of the coming generation, but being ready to go any day without fear and anxiety—that, in practice, is the spirit in which we are forced to live. It is not easy to be brave and keep the spirit alive, but it is imperative.[1]

In their despair, most Vietnam veterans I dealt with appeared to be living for the moment. Whether they did so irresponsibly or frivolously is another question; frivolity often serves as an escape valve. Had they resigned? I am not so sure, even though many of them said they had. *Resignation* means "patient submission, passive acceptance, acquiescence." This is not what I have found among the veterans. They are angry; they want things to be different. First and foremost they are angry with God. But that is good news because this

77

anger is a tacit admission of some intimacy with God. Thus, their anger with God combined with their desire for things to be different has positive implications for the future.

True, the members of my rap groups in Brainerd and St. Cloud may have at times *appeared* frivolous, irresponsible, or resigned in their anger. But the fact that they came to meetings of these groups at all and were concerned about each other, about politics, the street people, the refugees, or the future of their children indicated something else, namely, that while pretending to live for the moment, their concern was with the future. And when pressed they would admit to it, too.

One doesn't become a psychologist, a builder, a farmer, a social worker only to deal with one's own suffering or to feed oneself; one does it because there is another world out there, a world that contains a promise even though "all seems black," to use Bonhoeffer's words. But to the veterans emerging "out of the night" these promises are not synonymous with illusions. Theirs is a world come of age.

Bonhoeffer's *theologia crucis*, which was the central theme of chapter 6, this theology of the cross that calls for man's participation in God's suffering, is inseparably linked to this world coming of age. If the concept of the suffering God makes sense to veterans, then it follows that they will grasp the meaning of the term *mündige Welt*. In our interview, Eberhard Bethge proposed the idea that their experience has made them the vanguard of this godless grown-up world, a state to which the rest of their nation had not yet progressed. He saw the former soldiers' role as comparable to that of the German resistance in World War II, though the circumstances of the two groups differ vastly: both were given "a unique opportunity to do for [their] society what had not been done before," as Bethge said.

Bonhoeffer's curious notion of a world come of age has often been misunderstood. It denotes a world without the kind of god the veterans have jettisoned, in their case the "god of American mythology."[2] In his biography of Dietrich Bonhoeffer, Bethge points out that in using the phrase "coming of age" Bonhoeffer was thinking of the introductory statement of Immanuel Kant's *Was ist Aufklärung?* [*What Is Enlightenment?*] (1784). It says, "The Enlightenment is the emergence of man from immaturity that he is himself responsible for. Immaturity is the incapacity to use one's own intelligence without the guidance of another person." Bethge informs us that "Bonhoeffer now takes Kant's description of maturity as an essential element in his *theologia crucis.*"[3] In his letter from Tegel prison of 8 June 1944, Bonhoeffer writes,

> The movement that began about the thirteenth century . . . towards the autonomy of man (in which I should include the discovery of the laws by which the world lives and deals with itself in science, social and political matters, art, ethics, and religion) has in our time reached an undoubted completion. Man has learnt to deal with himself in all questions of importance without recourse to the 'working hypothesis' called 'God'. In questions of science, art, and ethics this has become an understood thing at which one now hardly dares to tilt. . . .
>
> The world that has become conscious of itself and the laws that govern its own existence has grown self-confident in what seems to us to be an uncanny way. . . . Efforts are made to prove to a world thus come of age that it cannot live without the tutelage of 'God'.[4] Even though there has been surrender on all secular problems, there still remain the so-called "ultimate questions"—death, guilt—to which only 'God' can give an answer, and because of which we need God and the church and the pastor. . . . But what if one day they no longer exist as such, if they too can be answered 'without God'?[5]

Surely, most Vietnam veterans who as a group have a highly developed sense of reality will agree with Bonhoeffer's affirmation of worldliness. For theirs is the world "that has become conscious of itself and the laws that govern its own existence."[6] In contrast to their fellow-countrymen, Bethge has suggested in an interview that their status is "after the event [of the world coming of age]." Their this-worldliness is surely not as shallow and banal as that of "the enlightened, the busy, the comfortable, and the lascivious," though it may not yet be "the profound this-worldliness characterized by discipline and the constant knowledge of death and resurrection."[7] For that would imply an understanding of God as the One to whom men go not only "in *their* distress" but also "in *his* distress."[8]

However, I have found that among those veterans who still believe in some kind of God—and they are in the majority—many could be persuaded by what has become one of Bonhoeffer's most famous statements, written four days before the unsuccessful attempt on Hitler's life:

> And we cannot be honest unless we recognize that we have to live in the

world *etsi deus non daretur* [as if there were no God]. And this is just
what we do recognize—before God! God himself compels us to recognize it. So our coming of age leads us to a true recognition of our
situation before God. God would have us know that we must live as
men who manage our lives without him. The God who is with us is the
God who forsakes us (Mark 15:34). The God who lets us live in the
world without the working hypothesis of God is the God before whom
we stand continually. Before God and with God we live without God.
God lets himself be pushed out of the world on to the cross. He is weak
and powerless in the world and that is precisely the way, the only way,
in which he is with us and helps us. Matt. 8:17 makes it quite clear that
Christ helps us, not by virtue of his omnipotence, but by virtue of his
weakness and suffering.[9]

The God as a working hypothesis in morals, politics, philosophy, and religion that Bonhoeffer refers to, a God who has been
"surmounted and abolished,"[10] is of course precisely the God the
veterans "flipped off" in Vietnam as opposed to the "hound who
pursues a person 'down the nights and down the days.'" Bonhoeffer
considers the world's coming of age a blessing, for it "has done away
with a false conception of God, opens up a way of seeing the God of
the Bible, who wins power and space in the world by his weakness."[11]

As I worked with Vietnam veterans on the psychiatric ward of the
Veterans Administration Medical Center in St. Cloud, I found an
unusual device to steer Vietnam veterans away from the God they
had "flipped off" and toward the "God of the Bible" that Bonhoeffer
writes about. These patients like to play cribbage. Its scores are kept
on a rectangular wooden pegboard which I used to make my point
about God.

When a veteran claimed that God and society had rejected and
abandoned him, I said, "Why don't you show me on the board where
society is and where you are?" Inevitably, he would arrange the pegs
representing society in one cluster on one end of the board, and the
peg representing himself on the other end. Then I gave him one
more peg and said, "This is God. Where is God's place?" The
veteran always placed the peg among the cluster, that is, among
society, whereupon I would ask, "What did the crowds shout on
Good Friday? Was it not, 'Let him be crucified'? Now, show me
again, where is God's place?" Almost automatically the veteran

would move the peg representing God next to the one representing himself, and when he realized what he had done he would accuse me of tricking him.

The theological corollary to this game is the reference to Bonhoeffer's theology of the cross: You see, as you are suffering with God in a godless world, God is suffering with you in a world you have experienced as godless. So what does that say to you? That God is a Vietnam vet!

Despite the sometimes brutal honesty I have found to be the mark of many Vietnam veterans, I never was chided for "chaplain bull," a favorite expression of theirs. For my interpretation of God seemed commensurate with their reality. It was a religionless one if we accept Bonhoeffer's definition of and opposition to religion as "that human activity that seeks to reach the beyond, to postulate a divinity, to invoke help and protection, in short: religion as self-justification."[12] To veterans sickened by the dichotomy between the religious beliefs of their childhood and the God-gone-AWOL in Vietnam, sickened by the inability of religious institutions to care for their wounded souls when they returned, Bonhoeffer has a liberating message: "We are moving towards a completely religionless time; people as they are now simply cannot be religious any more. Even those who honestly describe themselves as 'religious' do not in the least act upon it."[13]

According to Bethge, Bonhoeffer was "quite certain that the tasks of the future lay in this direction, i.e. that the Gospel should be freed from its traditional trammels and be understood and passed on, that it should, in other words, continue to live on in a 'non-religious' way."[14]

However, Bonhoeffer's terms, such as "non-religious" or "worldly re-interpretation" of the Gospel, must never be misused in an atheistic sense. His central concern is the presence of Christ in this world come of age; it is none other than the cross which allows for autonomy of mankind in the world:

> The cross of Christ is the cross of the reconciliation of the world with God. . . . The cross of atonement is the setting free for life before God in the midst of the godless world; it is the setting free for life in genuine worldliness. Jesus Christ imposes no alien law upon creation; but at the same time He does not tolerate any "autonomy" of creation in detachment from His commandment. The commandment of Jesus Christ,

the living Lord, sets creation free for the fulfillment of the law which is its own, that is to say, the law which is inherent in it by virtue of its having its origin, its goal and its essence in Jesus Christ. . . . Jesus Christ's claim to lordship, which is proclaimed by the Church, means at the same time emancipation of family, culture and government for the realization of their own essential character which has its foundation in Christ.[15]

The church as they know it, the church that has failed them, means little to virtually all Vietnam veterans I have met. It has no discernible part in the lives of those among them who endeavor to think and act "for the sake of the coming generation, but [are] ready to go any day without fear and anxiety." But Bonhoeffer has another kind of church in mind, a this-worldly church based solely on Christ's incarnation. Of that church he writes: "Church is no ideal, but reality in the world, a piece of worldliness. The worldliness of the church ensues from Christ's incarnation. Like Christ, church has become world."[16]

Into this this-worldly church the latent church of the Vietnam veterans must ultimately evolve, lest they have suffered in vain.

8

The Communion of Saints

OPTIMISM

It is wiser to be pessimistic; it is a way of avoiding disappointment and ridicule. . . . The essence of optimism is not its view of the present, but the fact that it is the inspiration of life and hope when others give in; it enables a man to hold his head high when everything else seems to be going wrong; it gives him strength to sustain reverses and yet to claim the future for himself instead of abandoning it to his opponent. . . . Optimism that is will for the future should never be despised, even if it is proved wrong a hundred times; it is health and vitality. . . . There are people who regard it as frivolous, and some Christians think it impious for anyone to hope and prepare for a better earthly future. They think that the meaning of present events is chaos, disorder, and catastrophe; and in resignation or pious escapism they surrender all responsibility for . . . future generations. It may be that the day of judgment will dawn tomorrow; in that case, we shall gladly stop working for a better future. But not before.[1]

Bonhoeffer's thoughts on optimism can be linked to the concept of the *sanctorum communio*. In defining this Christ working *as* community, Bonhoeffer has modified an idea advanced by G.W.F. Hegel in the early nineteenth century. According to Hegel, God exists as the community that is the dwelling place of the Holy Spirit.[2]

Bethge suggested that in communities such as the rap groups either Christ or the devil is present. According to Bethge, Christ goes into a desperate situation and endures it. If we apply Bonhoeffer's theology to this scenario, Christ works on the individual group member through his presence in all the others. When they challenge and judge one of their peers and then build him up again, it is in reality Christ who challenges, judges, and restores him. Acting as the group, Christ sets the individual limits and, in doing this, liberates that member from himself.

On the other hand, when the members only wallow in their own painful experiences, the devil is at work. The devil wants to drag the individual down; the devil wants him to fall deeper and deeper, Bethge explained. The wish to infect others is the essence of evil.

By Bethge's—and therefore Bonhoeffer's—definition, Christ was already present in the groups with which I worked. Their members did indeed challenge and judge each other, but never without building each other up again. Bethge interpreted this phenomenon as an excellent example of what Bonhoeffer meant by the term *Christus praesens:* When acting as a community, Christ always has two sides, the side of judgment and the side of the resurrection.

But this kind of presence does not yet qualify a rap group as a community of saints. As I discussed in chapter 4, it can be called a latent church, for the group is still unconscious of its own Christianity. However, if the Vietnam veterans are to have a major impact on their society, it is imperative for their latent church to grow into a manifest church fit for the world come of age, an optimistic church "with a will for the future, even if it is proved wrong a hundred times," a religionless church that belongs "wholly to the world [in which case] Christ is no longer an object of religion, but something quite different, really the Lord of the world."[3]

Where the Vietnam veterans are concerned, this kind of church, though wholly of the world, would also be a church of the catacombs, as opposed to the church that faintheartedly accommodates whims of the world and therefore presumably pays as little attention to their plight as it did to the suffering of Christ's followers, Jews, and others in Nazi Germany. For the catacombs is where they have been ever since their return to the United States which, ironically, they longingly called "the world" as they were trying to stay alive in the jungles and rice paddies of Vietnam.

THE DEVELOPING CHURCH

In Bonhoeffer's terminology, then, the *sanctorum communio* is the Church, the body of Christ. He exists and acts as this community. Shortly before his execution, Bonhoeffer developed this criterion:

"Church is the church only when it exists for others. . . . It must tell men of every calling what it means to live in Christ, to exist for others."[4] By these definitions some elements of a *sanctorum communio* are evident in the rap groups.

1. *The community clearly exists.* It distinguishes itself from both the society that rejected the returning soldiers *and* from the veterans who have not yet come 'out of the night' in that its members do not see "doing their own thing" as their raison d'être. This corresponds to Jay Rochelle's observation in his introduction to Bonhoeffer's *Spiritual Care:* "Christianity offers no place to 'do your own thing.' The aim of spiritual care is the integration of the person with the human community, beginning with one's relationship to God in the community of faith."[5]

2. *The community is not a selfish one.* It is loving, mutually supportive, spiritual, and looking beyond its members' predicaments. The veterans' actions support Rochelle's insight that "the greatest burden we must bear is that of another person's freedom."[6] That we become free to bear each other through the proclamation of Christ in our lives is another unresolved issue—like the relationship with God. Though they have never heard that "Christ takes form in the individual so that one becomes a 'little Christ' to the neighbor,"[7] they behave that way, and in this attitude are not limited just to the treatment of one another—as we have seen in their remarks about the street people (chapter 4) and in Vet 1's work with Indochinese refugees. This agrees with Bill Mahedy's observations: "The pain of the world, which [psychologist Peter] Marin believes is the burden of Vietnam vets, is shared by many others who are not vets but whose spiritual lives have taken on some of the same kind of scars. Those who have made the connection, between peace, justice, and their own spiritual lives—one meets them in parish groups, working in soup kitchens, helping refugees, searching for ways to move beyond war—have already taken this long step out of the darkness that always surrounds evil."[8]

3. *The community affirms its obligation to future generations.* As the Brainerd group discussed Bonhoeffer's passage on optimism, the following conversation took place:

Siemon-Netto: (pointing at individual veterans sitting around a circle) Now, you are doing an M.A. in psychology, and you are doing a B.A. in psychology, and you are in the building business, and you are still in the military as a reserve officer, and you are lecturing. Are you doing this strictly for self-gratification? Or are you not future oriented?

Vet 3: Well, I would guess that in order to get anything out of this [suffering], I'd have to be able to make it worthwhile for somebody else. Help somebody else out with this. Otherwise there is no meaning to any of this. Because I don't understand why this would even have been necessary, unless, of course, what [Bonhoeffer's] paper is saying is true: that what I have learned from this suffering I should be able to . . . give to other people so that they don't have to suffer as much.

Vet 4: We have to take our ounce of prevention and make damn sure that nobody else has to go through this bull again.

Vet 1: It is my observation of the Vietnam veterans, and myself included, [that they] sense a future of moving things ahead and improving things. And I think that one of the problems that we have when we get back in touch with the outside world is that there are so many people who are self-serving. I don't find that among the Vietnam veterans. They want to give of themselves because at one point they [were in] need of friends. I hear those other people pontificate, "I am a self-made man, no one has ever helped me" and all that kind of bull. But—we know that's not true. More or less we help each other.

4. *The community affirms life in this world.* The Brainerd group spoke most profoundly on the subject of insecurity and death. Bonhoeffer writes,

We surprise ourselves by the calmness with which we hear of the death of one of our contemporaries. . . . Fundamentally we feel that we really belong to death already, and that every new day is a miracle. It would probably not be true that we welcome death . . . ; we are too inquisitive for that. . . . We still love life, but I do not think that death can take us by surprise now. After what we have been through during the war, we hardly dare to admit that we should like death to come to us, not accidentally and suddenly through some trivial cause, but in the fullness of life and with everything at stake. It is we ourselves, and not outward circum-

stances, who make death what it can be, a death freely and voluntarily accepted.[9]

This is what Vet 2, the graduate student of psychology, said about this passage:

Vet 2: I underlined, "It would probably not be true that we welcome death," and I put a question mark by it. I wonder about the whole thing. I don't know. I might welcome death. I couldn't kill myself. I thought about it a lot, and when it came down to it I just . . . couldn't do it. Not because I didn't have balls enough, [but] because I would hurt my parents. I would hurt my brothers. You know, I have a lot of friends who would be bummed out. So I couldn't kill myself—because I didn't want to hurt anybody else. But if I were to be accidentally killed, well then, I don't know. Last winter the . . . dentist damn near killed me, and I was in intensive care and I damn near died. And they had machines all hooked up on me and IVs going in there and . . . I had a mind out of body experience where I was floating around and looking down on myself. And that was the best I have ever . . . felt in my life. I felt like I was dying and I was happy.

The existence of a loving and unselfish community with a sense of responsibility to future generations fulfills one of the criteria by which Bonhoeffer defines the *sanctorum communio*. But other characteristics suggest that the rap groups have not yet evolved into a community of saints.

1. *The community is exclusive.* The veterans still distrust outsiders, especially women, who are almost never admitted to group sessions; when they are, the atmosphere is inevitably tense. Most of the veterans I have worked with have one or even several divorces behind them. Their wrath is directed not at women in general, but specifically at American women whom they accuse of being self-centered, superficial, and insensitive to their suffering.

There are signs that these attitudes are changing. Several group members now enjoy happy marriages, often with women belonging to a generation that by virtue of its age cannot be blamed for the "Dear John" letters and other forms of rejection the veterans experienced. Still, the relationships are in many cases far from normal. For example, one veteran I have counseled individually told me that, although he now had a wonderful wife and two children, he always kept a packed suitcase under his bed to make sure that he could "take off at any given moment and never come back." He said he could not guarantee that this was not going to happen.

Clearly, if veterans are to have a decisive influence on their society, they must come to terms with all elements of that society. Otherwise they will not be a sanctorum communio; they will not be the nucleus of an *ekklēsia*, of a church for the world come of age; they will not be the moving force of a catholic, or whole, church. They will degenerate into an insignificant sect, and what Bethge called an historic opportunity will have been lost. The key word here, as in many other aspects of the drama of these veterans, is forgiveness.

2. *The community has an unresolved relationship with God; it is in a state of unfaith.* Though on the whole the veterans believe in a god, it is questionable whether this god is the God of Christianity, the God who suffers as we exercise our freedom to accept or reject God, who suffers with us in our estrangement which is sin. Though they may have recited the *Agnus Dei* on Sunday, the veterans never grasped the full meaning of Christ's redemptive achievement, namely, that he became the *peccator peccatorum* (the sinner of sinners), as Luther called him. Quoting Luther, Robert W. Bertram writes, "For our sake God made Christ to be sin," a "curse for us," or in the words of Isaiah, "numbered among the thieves." "By divine love sin was laid upon him." In fact, it *was* the divine love, his very willingness to be the *peccator peccatorum*, which before the law was the most sinful thing about him. And it was this "sinful" divine love, by compelling the law to attack him, which invalidated that law and its whole legalistic mode of predication, so that henceforth "there is no condemnation for those who are in Jesus Christ."[10]

Faith compels one to believe that the "spiritual darkness, as the vets have known it, [which] is really an overpowering awareness of the extent of human sin,"[11] will ultimately turn their latent church into a sanctorum communio. Though they often protest that they do not require it, their need to be forgiven *and to forgive* is clear to anyone who works with them. Frequently semantics hampers appropriate spiritual care for Vietnam veterans. Their often unconscious quest for forgiveness has nothing to do with whether or not they "did something wrong" in Vietnam. It is, rather, the consequence of what might even be termed a privilege: Unlike most of their contemporaries, they have been allowed to look into the abyss and thus have become overwhelmingly aware of human sin in the sense of estrangement from the Ground of Being. That they are privileged becomes apparent when we consider the phenomenon of "survivor guilt," which in theological terms is an overwhelming awareness of estrangement that turns the one who is stricken by it into a "little Christ," who in a sense is suffering for others.

THE NEED FOR FORGIVENESS

It is therefore imperative that the veterans be made aware of who Christ really is in this world come of age. One of Bonhoeffer's most significant insights is that the universal priesthood of all believers allows one member of a congregation to forgive the sins of another. Of course, "only he who has taken the sins upon himself can forgive them, namely Christ," Bonhoeffer writes, "but that means for us [that Christ's act of forgiving is performed through his presence in] his congregation, the *sanctorum communio*."[12] If we follow Bonhoeffer, then, the key to the issue of estrangement, raised by Paul Tillich and so deeply felt by the veterans, is to be found in John 20:23: "If you forgive the sins of any, they are forgiven; if you retain the sins of any, they are retained."

Thus, Bonhoeffer writes, "No proper spiritual care occurs without the forgiveness of sins."[13] Rochelle's variations on this theme read as if they had been written for the veterans:

The word of forgiveness comes to those who live life to the fullest and deepest, who engage in struggle at the extremes. Those who hate and those who love, those who desire order and those who live with chaos, those who weep and those who rejoice, those who celebrate and those who refuse to celebrate: they are some who are ready for the life in God proffered by forgiveness. Only to those who have known the grievous power of sin will the proclamation of forgiveness come as good news; the dead are those in need of the proclamation of resurrection. The church is not for those who feel themselves to be whole so much as for those who, having gone as far as they can under their own power, are prepared to risk the faith that there is a power beyond them in which they are personally fulfilled. The church is for those whose yearnings for self-transcendence and transformation crack on the knowledge that we who would transform ourselves are imperfect tools for the job and that we do not really know what we would like to become.[14]

But what is the church? Is the institution that has so dismally failed these men still a catholic church? Can it provide mission to them? Or will the drama of faith that is only beginning to unfold with the Vietnam veterans in the leading roles be played out in exactly the reverse: they will be the missionaries to the church of a world come of age? "I believe the act of trust in God made in the deepest agony of the soul is the most difficult of all religious acts; it is also the most Christlike," writes Mahedy. He continues, " 'Happy face' faith and love are authentic and may be sufficient if one never experiences the winter of the spirit. Vietnam veterans and others who have confronted the world's pervasive evil no longer have the luxury of swimming on the surface of religious life. Having been pulled into the depth, one must learn to swim underwater."[15]

Swimming underwater distinguishes, of course, the church in the catacombs of this world come of age: the church of Bonhoeffer and Martin Niemoeller in Nazi Germany, the church that survived the Cultural Revolution in China, the powerful and indestructible churches of Eastern Europe which often function in "subversive" cells parallel to the official church of which its faithful may or may not be members. In East Germany, for example, these Christian cells have infiltrated all walks of life. They exist in apartment buildings, factories, offices, even in the National People's Army. The members' modus operandi is a simple one: they bear witness by living and acting as Christians—by living their Christian lives to the fullest in a world come of age. In doing so they attract their neighbors' attention; they become missionaries.[16]

Churches thus swimming underwater often fit Edgar Krentz's description of the egalitarian church of Matthew, that is, an "unstructured community of equals." Krentz writes, "There is not respect of persons in the Matthean church. All who respond to the proclamation and become disciples become equals. That response, which includes confession to Jesus, is all that is asked. . . . The church is unstructured. It has no distinctions of class or office."[17]

If the latent church of the veterans is to develop into a sanctorum communio, it will be Matthean in format, and ministry to the veterans must be mindful of this. In a rap group the former colonel equals the former private; each is called to task and comforted by the other. The job at hand is to transform that group into a church. The fact that they are all different should be no impediment to this endeavor. The church is not a club of like-minded members. Those tied together in the Body of Christ need not even like each other. In Rochelle's words, "Community is not the same as camaraderie."[18]

But where the sanctorum communio of the veterans is concerned, a community in which the colonel equals the private, there is no room for clerical titles, vestments, or rites. There is no room for "chaplain bull" and sanctimony. Those who wish to proclaim to the ones who have stood at the abyss must be prepared to do so in four-letter words. And if the institutional church wants to make sure that, for all the obscenities, there be no question that the content of the proclamation is orthodox, it must overcome its bureaucratic inhibitions and swiftly begin training some of the most unorthodox ministers in its history. Candidates will have to be found from among the veterans themselves, especially those who had been medics in Vietnam (see chap. 7).

Is there a chance for the veterans' return to faith? Bonhoeffer's observations on faith and obedience suggest that there is.

> . . . Only the obedient believe. If we are to believe, we must obey a concrete command. Without this preliminary step of obedience, our faith will only be pious humbug, and lead us to grace which is not costly. Everything depends on the first step. It has a unique quality of its own. The first step of obedience makes Peter leave his nets, and later get out of the ship; it calls upon the young man to leave his riches. Only this new existence can make faith possible. This first step must be regarded as an external work which effects the change from one existence to another. It is a step within everybody's capacity, for it lies within the limits of the natural law . . . and in that sphere man is free. Although Peter cannot achieve his own conversion, he can leave his nets.[19]

Vietnam veterans have risked their lives in obedience to man's law. They can be convinced to be obedient in order to be granted the faith of which it can be said, "The passage from darkness to light is God's free gift and not ours to take."[20]

What I propose here is not the establishment of a Christian sect of Vietnam veterans, however, but a pivotal organ of the Body of Christ. Those veterans who as underwater swimmers are prepared to suffer with God in a godless world will do for the church in America what Christian base groups in East Germany are doing for the official church in that country: They may not show up in traditional places of worship for a long time, yet they will be a new impetus for the church reforming itself (*ecclesia semper reformanda*). It is up to the church to make use of this opportunity. A fainthearted church that attempts to thwart its decline in membership only by catering to the perceived sufferings of the comfortable instead of allowing itself to be reformed by those who have suffered genuinely and persistently for such a long time may not have too great a future in a world come of age.

"Optimism is will for the future," writes Bonhoeffer. It is not a banal kind of optimism he is talking about. Maybe what we expect from the veterans is not optimism at all. After all, Martin Heidegger calls optimism and its opposite, pessimism, childish categories. As a vanguard of a world come of age, the veterans cannot really be optimistic according to Heidegger's definition of the term. Once they have received the gift of faith they are more likely to provide the opposite of the despair they have suffered. And that opposite is hope, which counts of course, together with faith and charity, among the highest of Christian virtues.

Conclusion

ARE WE STILL OF ANY USE?

We have been silent witnesses of evil deeds; we have been drenched by many storms; we have learnt the arts of equivocation and pretence; experience has made us suspicious of others and kept us from being truthful and open; intolerable conflicts have worn us down and even made us cynical. Are we still of any use? What we shall need is not geniuses, or cynics, or misanthropes, or clever tacticians, but plain, honest, straightforward men. Will our inward power of resistance be strong enough, and our honesty with ourselves remorseless enough, for us to find our way back to simplicity and straightforwardness?[1]

Are the Vietnam veterans still of any use? If Dietrich Bonhoeffer were alive today he would surely ask: "How could they *not* be of any use if they have suffered so much?" Let us remember Bonhoeffer's thoughts on the importance of suffering in human development:

We have to learn that personal suffering is a more effective key, a more rewarding principle for exploring the world in thought and action than personal good fortune.[2]

In my twenty-five years of close involvement with the United States I have observed with great sadness how this nation, which in the eyes of its friends has clearly been called to world leadership, will not free itself from what one might call a *Tin Drum* syndrome; like the little boy in Günter Grass's most famous novel it refuses to grow up. And this is no longer endearing because it puts future generations and indeed humanity at risk.

Self-indulgence is perhaps the most troublesome aspect of a Tin

93

Drum society waiting to be reformed by men whose pain has taken them across the threshold of the world come of age. Childish self-indulgence manifests itself in our habit of throwing away what seems boring and is not desired at any given moment.

Like spoiled and petulant children we throw away plastic bags, edible food, allies, soldiers returning from war. The list can be continued ad infinitum: Public transport systems, such as passenger trains, were discarded without any consideration for the needs of future generations. Grandparents, whose wisdom and experience were throughout history and in every culture considered critical to the upbringing of children, are being dismissed from family structures and sent off to play shuffleboard in the sun.

One of contemporary America's greatest dilemmas, the mass destruction of unborn life, must also be considered in this context. As a sinister irony would have it, abortions were legalized in 1973, the same year the United States brought its last combatants home from Vietnam. Between then and the end of 1988 an estimated 23 million pregnancies were legally terminated and the killing continues at a rate of 1.6 million a year. Abortion is by no means an exclusively American phenomenon, but it is more pronounced in this country than in comparable societies overseas.

"Are we still of any use?" It is difficult to see how those who have suffered so much from being slandered as baby killers will *not* have something to say to a society that has already wiped out the equivalent of almost the entire population of Canada—not on military orders or at the behest of some totalitarian regime, but as an "act of free will," as Bonhoeffer would phrase it.

The Tin Drum syndrome manifests itself in a myriad of other ways as well. Here is the richest land on earth giddily moving from fad to fad and ideology to ideology. Here it is, drugging itself, pointing a finger accusingly at the foreign caterers to this self-indulgence while ignoring until recently its own complicity in the use of mind-expanding drugs as a substitute for God.

"Are we still of any use?" Doubtless, those who drugged themselves to forget pain and fear will have something useful to say and do in a society that drugs itself often for no other reason than not wanting to face the realities of a world come of age.

In chapter 8 I discussed two forms of optimism. One is

Bonhoeffer's kind. It is rooted in history and is "will for the future." It is the optimism of the mature who have no illusions but do have the virtue of hope. And then there is the banal, the "silly, cowardly kind of optimism" without reference to history or any other precedent, and therefore without a sense of responsibility for the future. It is the optimism of the "me" generation and of those who are "doing their own thing." It is an optimism that always seeks instant solutions at the expense of those who depend on us, who follow us. It is Tin Drum optimism, the optimism of the immature.

Tin Drum optimism can be found across the political spectrum. It creates the illusion that to do nothing or to do what is expedient will actually solve problems. Tin Drum optimism comes with the self-righteous veneer and voice inflection of those who always find an excuse for not taking what Bonhoeffer calls "responsible action in a bold venture of faith." In an idolatrous reference to freedom, gun controls are not enforced, affordable medical insurance for the entire population is not provided, AIDS tests and drug tests are not made compulsory where reason says that they should be. The Tin Drum syndrome becomes apparent in the neglect of the infrastructure as evidenced by collapsing bridges, hazardous dams, an interstate highway system that urgently requires a major overhaul, and a desperate need for new airports and sewage plants.

God's demand for "responsible action in a bold venture of faith" is clearly not met by the world's richest nation which in its self-indulgence passes on such a huge burden to the next generation without even training it to cope with the consequences. Bonhoeffer, whose concern for the next generation dominated so much of his literary and theological work, would find little solace at the sight of a nation which has so thoroughly damaged its educational system that Baltimore eighth-graders could not find their own land on a globe and young Texas Hispanics were unable to name the country that lies on their state's southern border.

There is stark contrast between a laissez-faire society that neglects to provide for its own future and the underwater swimmers who have themselves experienced the dire consequences of the lack of concern for that future. It is a contrast between the "before and after," as Bethge would say, a contrast between those who do not yet live in a world come of age and those who have been forced into it.

Not just faith, but logic, too, compels one to believe that a Tin Drum society's inevitable transition from its state of banal optimism to a hopeful world come of age will occur with the help of qualified guides. And their chief qualification will be a maturity that comes from having looked into the abyss, from having profoundly experienced suffering.

Christians who believe in a Lord of history also know that God has provided other such guides as history has unfolded. Thus it seems reasonable to suggest that this task may fall to these veterans, "plain, honest, and straightforward" men who trained twice as long as it takes to educate a Jesuit priest. Tin Drum thinking assumes that since they are now in their forties and fifties they are too old to make a change. A world come of age has a different yardstick: the banal optimism of the young will count little if measured against what might be seen as the longest seminary education in our time, an education that lasted two decades and featured *suffering* as its principal course.

It is an education which will surely lead to the recognition that suffering is an act of solidarity with the God who shows solidarity with us by suffering for us, a God who is never Absent Without Leave.

Notes

INTRODUCTION

1. Title 10 of the U.S. Code prescribes prison terms of one month to three years for Unauthorized Absence (section 885) and even the death penalty for desertion in times of war (section 886). A deserter is a soldier who intends to stay away permanently.

2. Arthur Kuhne, coordinator of the Mental Hygiene Clinic, VA Medical Center, St. Cloud, Minnesota, in interview with author (June, 1987). Hereafter cited as interview with Arthur Kuhne.

3. "Roche Report," *Frontiers of Psychiatry* (Nutley), vol. 10, no. 5 (1980): 12–13.

4. James Tuorila, psychologist at VA Medical Center, in interview with author (March, 1988).

5. Edwin Randolph Parson, "The Reparation of the Self: Clinical and Theoretical Dimensions in the Treatment of Vietnam Veterans," *Journal of Contemporary Psychotherapy,* vol. 14, no. 1 (1984): 4–5.

6. Victor J. DeFazio and Nicholas J. Pascussi, "Return to Ithaca: A Perspective on Marriage and Love in Post-Traumatic Stress Disorder," *Journal of Contemporary Psychotherapy,* vol. 14, no. 1 (1984): 76–78.

7. Interview with Arthur Kuhne.

8. KZ is the German acronym for concentration camp.

9. J. Ingram Walker and Jesse O. Cavenar, "Vietnam Veterans: Their Problems Continue," *Journal of Nervous and Mental Disease,* vol. 170, no. 3 (1987): 174–79. Hereafter cited as Walker.

10. Herman Wiersinga, "The Part of Suffering in the Theology of Dietrich Bonhoeffer," lecture delivered at the annual meeting of the International Bonhoeffer Society, Oxford, England, 1980.

11. Dietrich Bonhoeffer, "After Ten Years," in *Letters and Papers from Prison,* ed. Eberhard Bethge (New York: Macmillan Co., 1972), 17.

12. Victor E. Frankl, *Man's Search for Meaning* (Boston: Beacon Press, 1962), 10.

13. Terrence Des Pres, *The Survivor: An Anatomy of Life in the Death Camps* (New York: Oxford University Press, 1976), 200.

14. Bethge in interview with author (Bonn, December 1987).

15. Bonhoeffer, *Letters and Papers from Prison*, 3–17. As Eberhard Bethge explained in our interview, this paper was aimed not specifically at theologians but at members of the resistance against Hitler, who came from diverse walks of life. Among them were officers, civil servants, lawyers, and academics. Although the situation to which "After Ten Years" addresses itself was ostensibly quite different from that of the Vietnam veterans, it nevertheless reads as if it had been written with their plight in mind. They, too, had their times stolen from them. Bonhoeffer's comforting words that "God can bring good out of evil, even out of the greatest evil" are as pertinent to them as they were to the resistance in World War II. The same holds true for the appeal not to despise the kind of optimism that "is will for the future," and indeed to work for a better future. "Are we still of any use?" Bonhoeffer asks with his fellow conspirators in mind. The resounding Yes, Bethge suggests, applies no less to the Vietnam veterans than it did to the valiant men who tried to put an end to the Nazi tyranny in Germany.

16. Robert Jay Lifton, "Advocacy and Corruption in the Healing Profession," in *Stress Disorders Among Vietnam Veterans*, ed. Charles R. Figley (New York: Brunner/Mazel, 1978), 212.

17. Walker and Cavenar, "Vietnam Veterans: Their Problems Continue," 178.

18. American Psychiatric Association, *Diagnostic and Statistical Manual of Mental Disorders*, 3d ed. (Washington, D.C.: American Psychiatric Association, 1980), 236–38.

19. Emanuel Tanay, "The Dear John Syndrome During the Vietnam War," *Diseases of the Nervous System* (March, 1976): 165–67.

20. Helmut Thielicke, *Das Gebet, das die Welt umspannt* (Stuttgart: Quell Verlag, 1980), 109.

21. William P. Mahedy, *Out of the Night* (New York: Ballantine Books, 1986), 115.

22. Ibid., 116.

23. Douglas John Hall, *God and Human Suffering* (Minneapolis: Augsburg Publishing House, 1986), 114.

24. Bonhoeffer, *Letters and Papers from Prison*, 160.

25. Paul Tillich, *Systematic Theology*, vol. 3 (Chicago: University of Chicago Press, 1963), 153.

26. Dietrich Bonhoeffer, *Sanctorum Communio* (Munich: Chr. Kaiser Verlag, 1986), 126 (my translation).

CHAPTER 1. THE STOLEN TIME

1. Bonhoeffer, *Letters and Papers from Prison*, 3.

2. Eberhard Bethge in interview with author (December, 1987).

3. Discussion with Vietnam veterans' rap group (February, 1988).
4. Mahedy, *Out of the Night*, 62.
5. Ibid., 65.
6. As this particular section of Bonhoeffer's essay seems singularly tailor-made to the situation of the German resistance of the 1940s, I am taking a literary liberty by using only the opening line as an excuse to outline the veterans' dilemma in detail.
7. Bonhoeffer, *Letters and Papers from Prison*, 3.
8. Walker and Cavenar, "Vietnam Veterans: Their Problems Continue," 175.
9. Melodie van Kampen, Charles G. Watson et al., "The Definition of Post-Traumatic Stress Disorder in Alcoholic Vietnam Veterans," *Journal of Nervous and Mental Disease*, vol. 174, no. 3 (1986): 135.
10. Kuhne in interview with author (April, 1988).
11. B. Bower, "Deadly Aftermath for Viet Nam Vets," *Science News* (Feb. 21, 1987): 117.
12. R. P. Grinker and J. P. Spiegel, *Men Under Stress* (New York: McGraw Hill, 1963), 104.
13. A. S. Blank, discussion of papers on the psychological problems of Vietnam Veterans, annual meeting of the American Psychiatric Association, San Francisco (1980).
14. F. Downs, "Vietnam Veterans Desperately Need Help," *Center Magazine*, no. 12 (1979): 47–48.
15. I am indebted to a comment by Paul Bauermeister, a theologian and psychologist, on this subject. He called this a "failure of military psychiatry" and pointed out that in World War II this soldier would have spent one month being debriefed on a troop ship with other combat veterans.
16. Mahedy, *Out of the Night*, 47.

CHAPTER 2. ENCOUNTERING EVIL

1. Bonhoeffer, *Letters and Papers from Prison*, 4.
2. Mahedy, *Out of the Night*, 110.
3. See Richard M. Nixon, *The Real War* (New York: Warner Books, 1980), 39.
4. Peter Braestrup, *Big Story* (Garden City, N.Y.: Anchor Press, 1978), 214.
5. Bonhoeffer, *Letters and Papers from Prison*, 4.
6. Mahedy, *Out of the Night*, 115.
7. Ibid., 111.
8. Ibid., 113.
9. The term "fragging" meant the killing of officers or NCOs. The term owes its origin to the throwing of fragmentation devices into the victim's

quarters, which was the most frequently used way of getting rid of a superior.

10. Bonhoeffer, *Letters and Papers from Prison*, 5.

11. Peter Marin, "Living in Moral Pain," *Psychology Today* (November, 1981):79.

12. Mahedy, *Out of the Night*, 115.

13. Paul Tillich, *Systematic Theology*, vol. 2 (Chicago: University of Chicago Press, 1957), 47.

14. Ibid.

15. Mahedy, *Out of the Night*, 5.

16. Bonhoeffer, *Letters and Papers from Prison*, 5.

17. Paul Tillich, *The Shaking of the Foundation* (New York: Charles Scribner's Sons, 1948), 147–48.

18. Mahedy, *Out of the Night*, 225.

CHAPTER 3. MAKING CHOICES

1. Bonhoeffer, *Letters and Papers from Prison*, 5.

2. Eberhard Bethge, *Dietrich Bonhoeffer* (New York: Harper & Row, 1970), 530.

3. Bonhoeffer, *Letters and Papers from Prison*, 6.

4. Mahedy, *Out of the Night*, 9.

5. Bonhoeffer, *Letters and Papers from Prison*, 7.

6. Mahedy, *Out of the Night*, 21.

7. Vet 4 is referring to Senator Albert Gore, who at the time was a candidate for the Democratic party's nomination for the presidency.

8. Mahedy, *Out of the Night*, 91.

9. According to Tillich, the Spiritual Community actualizes the New Being in Jesus. Tillich, *Systematic Theology*, vol. 3, 123.

10. Ibid., 15.

11. Ibid.

12. Dietrich Bonhoeffer, "Thoughts on the Day of the Baptism of Dietrich Wilhelm Rüdiger Bethge," in *Letters and Papers from Prison*, 300.

CHAPTER 4. WHERE AMERICA FAILED ITS VETERANS

1. Bonhoeffer, *Letters and Papers from Prison*, 8.

2. Mahedy, *Out of the Night*, 177–78.

3. John Fergueson, "A Man of Sorrows, Familiar with Suffering." Interview in *The Olympia Churchman* (July/August 1985): 6.

4. Ibid.

5. Bonhoeffer, *Letters and Papers from Prison*, 9.

6. Stephen Howard, "The Vietnam Warrior: His Experience and Implications for Psychotherapy," *American Journal of Psychotherapy*, vol. 30 (January 1976): 128.

7. Emanuel Tanay, "The Dear John Syndrome During the Vietnam War," 165.

8. Bernard Fall, *The Two Vietnams* (New York: Vintage Press, 1968), 234; and Robert F. Turner, *Vietnamese Communism* (Stanford: Hoover Institution Press, 1975), 9.

9. The formerly American, now Soviet, naval base of Cam Ranh Bay is now thought to be a cornerstone in the Soviet Union's Pacific strategy. According to U.S. military planners it poses a major threat to the state of Hawaii, site of CINCPAC, the headquarters of the U.S. forces in the Pacific. (Interview with U.S. military intelligence officers, Honolulu, March 1983.)

10. Had a similar media policy been in place in World War II, American civilians would have learned about the damage caused by the Allied advance in Europe, but little about Nazi extermination camps and the Gestapo terror in both Germany and the German-held territories.

11. Mahedy, *Out of the Night*, 41.

12. Myra MacPherson, *Long Time Passing: Vietnam and the Haunted Generation* (New York: Doubleday & Co., 1984), 83.

13. Mahedy, *Out of the Night*, 39.

14. Lenny Roberts reported these incidents in an international forum at LSTC on January 24, 1988.

15. Timothy C. Sims, "Gulag and Kyrie," *LCA Partners*, vol. 5, no. 3 (Fall 1985): 10.

16. Bonhoeffer, *Letters and Papers from Prison*, 9–10.

CHAPTER 5. GOOD FROM EVIL

1. "Immanent Righteousness" and "A Few Articles of Faith on the Sovereignty of God in History" are two separate sections in Bonhoeffer's Essay "After Ten Years." In this paper I merge them into one because the insights they contain may be applied to one single aspect of the veterans' journey from suffering to influencing America's destiny.

2. Bonhoeffer, *Letters and Papers from Prison*, 11.

3. Kurt Dietrich Schmidt, *Kirchengeschichte* (Göttingen: Vandenhoeck & Ruprecht, 1960), 55. "[Paulus'] Hineinstellung des Evangeliums in die griechische Geisteswelt war gewiss Voraussetzung für den Erfolg, missionarische Grosstat."

4. Bonhoeffer, *Letters and Papers from Prison*, 10.

5. This is one of the most astonishing discoveries I have made while living as a freelance correspondent in France for ten years. That POW experiences had dramatically changed the views of each other held by Germans and

Notes

Frenchmen has been confirmed in interviews with scores of former prisoners, both French and German, as well as their families, and officials of both countries. There has even been a film made about this subject.

6. Dietrich Bonhoeffer, *Ethics* (New York: Macmillan Co., 1955), 216.
7. Ibid., 130.
8. Mahedy, *Out of the Night*, 160.
9. Stephen T. Davis, "Free Will and Evil," in *Encountering Evil*, ed. Stephen T. Davis (Atlanta: John Knox Press, 1981), 70.
10. Tillich, *Shaking of the Foundation*, 147–48.
11. Hall, *God and Human Suffering*, 187.
12. Bonhoeffer, *Letters and Papers from Prison*, 11.

CHAPTER 6. MAKING SENSE OF THE VETERANS' PAIN

1. Bonhoeffer, *Letters and Papers from Prison*, 13.
2. Dean W. Bard, associate vice president, Lutheran School of Theology at Chicago, in a sermon preached on 2 March 1988 at LSTC.
3. Ibid.
4. Mahedy, *Out of the Night*, 116.
5. "Apology of the Augsburg Confession [Article II. Original Sin]," *The Book of Concord*, trans. and ed. Theodore G. Tappert (Philadelphia: Fortress Press, 1959), 101.
6. Interview with Arthur Kuhne.
7. Mahedy, *Out of the Night*, 99.
8. Dietrich Bonhoeffer, *Spiritual Care* (Philadelphia: Fortress Press, 1985), 62.
9. Mahedy, *Out of the Night*, 116.
10. Ibid., 205.
11. Ibid., 215.
12. Tillich, *Systematic Theology*, vol. 2, 48.
13. Ibid.
14. Anselm's doctrine holds that humans owe the Creator total response but withhold it, which is sin. We thus dishonor God and disrupt the order of creation. Just by returning to obedience humankind will not be able to pay back for past sins. Restitution to the divine honor can only be made by paying back more than the total obedience owed. This is done by Christ. As sinless God-man it is not incumbent on him to die. His death is worth more than anything that is not God. So great a sacrifice deserves a reward. But a God-man needs no reward. So he gives it to those for whom he became incarnate. They will be saved.

Abelard was the first to introduce the moral influence theory. It sees Christ as the one who persevered unto death in instructing in the way of love, binding humankind to himself so that we should fear nothing in the exercise of love. Over the centuries, this theory has been put forward in many variations. To some, humans are incapable of doing what is demanded of them and so need a substitute. Others feel that man needs only encouragement and guidance, which Jesus provides.

Aulen's theory is one of a dramatic battle between Christ and demonic forces. Christ, through whom God works in this battle, is victorious and releases the enslaved mankind.

15. Gerhard O. Forde, "The Work of Christ," in *Christian Dogmatics* (Philadelphia: Fortress Press, 1984), 47.

16. Dietrich Bonhoeffer, *Gesammelte Schriften*, vol. 5, ed. Eberhard Bethge (Munich: Chr. Kaiser Verlag, 1972), 421.

17. Ibid., 420.

18. Ibid., 421.

19. Mahedy, *Out of the Night*, 165.

20. Forde, "The Work of Christ," 55.

21. Jürgen Moltmann, *Der gekreuzigte Gott* (Munich: Chr. Kaiser Verlag, 1972), 265, my trans.

22. Forde, "The Work of Christ," 52.

23. Kazoh Kitamori, *Theologie des Schmerzes Gottes* (Göttingen: Vandenhoeck & Ruprecht, 1932), 37 (my trans.).

24. Ibid., 36.

25. Ibid., 147.

26. Dietrich Bonhoeffer, *The Cost of Discipleship* (New York: Macmillan Co., 1959), 80.

27. Ibid.

38. Bonhoeffer, *Ethics*, 82.

29. Bonhoeffer, *The Cost of Discipleship*, 77.

30. Ibid., 78.

31. Ibid., 79.

32. Moltmann, *Der gekreuzigte Gott*, 265.

33. Ibid., 266.

34. Bonhoeffer, *Letters and Papers from Prison*, 166.

CHAPTER 7. A WORLD COME OF AGE

1. Bonhoeffer, *Letters and Papers from Prison*, 14.

2. Mahedy, *Out of the Night*, 215.

3. Bethge, *Dietrich Bonhoeffer*, 770.

4. Please note Bonhoeffer's use of quotation marks here, which signify that to Bonhoeffer this 'God' is not the real God.

5. Bonhoeffer, *Letters and Papers from Prison*, 325.

6. Ibid.

7. Ibid., 369.

8. Bonhoeffer, "Notes," in *Letters and Papers from Prison*, 343 (my emphasis).

9. Bonhoeffer, *Letters and Papers from Prison*, 360.

10. Ibid.

11. Ibid., 361.

12. Bethge, *Dietrich Bonhoeffer*, 775.

13. Bonhoeffer, *Letters and Papers from Prison*, 279.

14. Bethge, *Dietrich Bonhoeffer*, 774.

15. Bonhoeffer, *Ethics*, 297.

16. Bonhoeffer, *Gesammelte Schriften*, vol. 5, 270 (my trans.).

CHAPTER 8. THE COMMUNION OF SAINTS

1. Bonhoeffer, *Letters and Papers from Prison*, 15.

2. G.W.F. Hegel, *Sämtliche Werke*, ed. G. Lasson, vol. 14, part 3, p. 198.

3. Bonhoeffer, *Letters and Papers from Prison*, 281.

4. Ibid., 382.

5. Bonhoeffer, *Spiritual Care*, 24.

6. Ibid., 9.

7. Ibid., 7.

8. Mahedy, *Out of the Night*, 211.

9. Bonhoeffer, *Letters and Papers from Prison*, 16.

10. Robert W. Bertram, "How Our Sins Were Christ's: A Study in Luther's *Galatians* (1531)," in *The Promising Tradition*, ed. Edward H. Schroeder (St. Louis: Seminex Press, 1978), 7–21.

11. Mahedy, *Out of the Night*, 115.

12. Bonhoeffer, *Sanctorum Communio*, 126 (my trans.).

13. Bonhoeffer, *Spiritual Care*, 57.

14. Ibid., 16.

15. Mahedy, *Out of the Night*, 16.

16. Information from my research in East Germany, 1975–80.

17. Edgar Krentz, "The Egalitarian Church of Matthew," *Currents in Theology and Mission* 4 (1977): 333–41.

18. Bonhoeffer, *Spiritual Care*, 14.

19. Bonhoeffer, *The Cost of Discipleship*, 55.

20. Mahedy, *Out of the Night*, 217.

CONCLUSION

1. Bonhoeffer, *Letters and Papers from Prison*, 16.

2. Ibid., 17.

Selected Bibliography

THEOLOGY

Bethge, Eberhard. *Dietrich Bonhoeffer.* New York: Harper & Row, 1970.

Bonhoeffer, Dietrich. *Act and Being.* New York: Octagon Books, 1983.

————. *The Cost of Discipleship.* Edited by Eberhard Bethge. New York: Macmillan Co., 1959.

————. *Ethics.* Edited by Eberhard Bethge. New York: Macmillan Co., 1955.

————. *Gesammelte Schriften.* Edited by Eberhard Bethge. Vol. 5. Munich: Chr. Kaiser, 1972.

————. *Letters and Papers from Prison.* Edited by Eberhard Bethge. New York: Macmillan Co., 1972.

————. *Sanctorum Communio.* Munich: Chr. Kaiser, 1986.
In this work Bonhoeffer develops his concept of Christ acting as community.

————. *Spiritual Care.* Philadelphia: Fortress Press, 1985.

Hall, Douglas John. *God and Human Suffering.* Minneapolis: Augsburg Publishing House, 1986.

Kitamori, Kazoh. *Theologie des Schmerzes Gottes.* Göttingen: Vandenhoeck & Ruprecht, 1932.

McGill, Arthur C. *Suffering.* Philadelphia: Westminster Press, 1982.

Mahedy, William P. *Out of the Night.* New York: Ballantine Books, 1986.
Written by a priest who served as a chaplain in Vietnam and has worked extensively with veterans. This book is a true rarity in its unsparing confrontation of the ultimate problem of human existence and its witness to the magnificently stubborn regenerative power of the human spirit. The author courageously addresses the theological and pastoral issues created by the Vietnam war and experienced by its veterans.

Moltmann, Jürgen. *Der gekreuzigte Gott.* Munich: Chr. Kaiser Verlag, 1972.

Tillich, Paul. *Systematic Theology,* vol 3. Chicago: University of Chicago Press, 1963.
In this volume Tillich deals extensively with his concept of the latent church.

Selected Bibliography

PSYCHOLOGY

Bower, B. "Deadly Aftermath for Vietnam Vets." *Science News*, February 21, 1987.

De Fazio, Victor J. and Nicholas Pascussi. "Return to Ithaca: A Perspective on Marriage and Love in Post-Traumatic Stress Disorder." *Journal of Contemporary Psychotherapy*, vol. 14, no. 1 (1984).

Des Pres, Terrence. *The Survivor: An Anatomy of Life in the Death Camps.* New York: Oxford University Press, 1976.

Figley, Charles R., ed. *Stress Disorder Among Vietnam Veterans.* New York: Brunner/Mazel, 1978.

Frankl, Victor E. *Man's Search for Meaning.* Boston: Beacon Press, 1962.

Grinker, R. P. and J. P. Spiegel. *Men Under Stress.* New York: McGraw Hill, 1963.

Howard, Stephen. "The Vietnam Warrior: His Experience and Implications for Psychotherapy." *American Journal for Psychotherapy*, vol. 30, no. 1 (January 1976).

Kohlberg, Lawrence. *The Philosophy of Moral Development.* San Francisco: Harper & Row, 1981.

———. *The Psychology of Moral Development.* San Francisco: Harper & Row, 1984.

Marin, Peter. "Living in Moral Pain." *Psychology Today*, vol. 15, no. 11 (November 1981).

Parson, Edwin Randolph. "The Reparation of the Self: Clinical and Theoretical Dimensions in the Treatment of Vietnam Veterans." *Journal of Contemporary Psychotherapy*, vol. 14, no. 1 (1984).

Sims, Timothy Calhoun. "Gulag and Kyrie." *LCA Partners*, vol. 5, no. 3 (June 1983).

Sonnenberg, Stephen M., Arthur S. Blank, Jr., and John A. Talbott. *The Trauma of War: Stress and Recovery in Vietnam Veterans.* Washington, D.C.: American Psychiatric Press, 1988.

Tanay, Emanuel, "The Dear John Syndrome During the Vietnam War." *Diseases of the Nervous System* (March 1976).

Walker, J. Ingram and Jesse O. Cavenar. "Vietnam Veterans: Their Problems Continue." *Journal of Nervous and Mental Disease*, vol. 170, no. 3 (1987).

ON VIETNAM

Braestrup, Peter. *Big Story.* Garden City, N.Y.: Anchor Press, 1978.

Capps, Walter. *The Unfinished War: Vietnam and the American Conscience.* Boston: Beacon Press, 1982.
The author uses historical and analytic tools to relate his extensive first-

hand knowledge of Vietnam veterans and make the case that Vietnam is an unfinished war in the American conscience. As such, he believes, the war presents a real danger that history will repeat itself as America's political and religious leaders advocate a return to outmoded ideals. The book has a comprehensive bibliography.

Caputo, Philip. *A Rumor of War.* New York: Holt, Rinehart & Winston, 1977; reprint edition, New York: Ballantine Books, 1978.

Written by a Marine Corps veteran. One of the great books to come out of the Vietnam war.

Fall, Bernard. *The Two Vietnams.* New York: Vintage Press, 1968.

A classic; considered compulsory reading by foreign correspondents and diplomats serving in Vietnam. This book provides a wealth of information on Vietnam's history, its repeated divisions, its wars, and the events that finally led to the victory of the communists. The author, a French scholar of Austrian descent, was involved in the French Indochina war. He did not live to see the fall of Saigon. He was killed when he stepped on a mine in 1968.

Herr, Michael. *Dispatches.* New York: Avon Books, 1978.

Karnow, Stanley. *Vietnam: A History.* New York: Viking Press, 1983.

Turner, Robert F. *Vietnamese Communism.* Stanford: Hoover Institution Press, 1975.

It was one of the strange phenomena of the Vietnam war that the nature and history of the adversary received little attention from the American media. This scholarly book probes deeply the backgrounds of Ho Chi Minh and his collaborators and proves that he had been a Comintern agent since the early 1920s.